Acclai

"This book will help every owner understand the true reality of condo and HOA living."

– Florida State Representative Julio Robaina

"A riveting work that condo and HOA owners everywhere will identify with."

– Jan Bergemann, President, Cyber Citizens for Justice (CCFJ.net)

"You are to be commended for your courage, degree of caring and commitment."

– Val Lucier, Florida's First Condo Election Monitor and Author of *Condo Board Revolt!*

"Thank you for your wonderful contributions to this important issue."

– Attorney Barry Boca, Florida

"Any victim of Condo or HOA enforcement who fails to read this book has only himself/herself to blame."

– Dr. David I. Goldenberg, Economist and Author of *Creating Condo & Home Owner Association Documents*

"This book gives me the encouragement I need."

– Phyllis W., Florida

"I'd hit rock bottom. I can't wait for your next edition."

– E. S., Miami

"I see light at the end of the tunnel. You have given me hope!"

– Florence G, Boca Raton

"I think what you did is wonderful. If I had your book, I would not have made such mistakes."

– Yolanda A, Florida

DEFEND YOUR
CONDO & HOMEOWNER
RIGHTS!

Defend Your Condo & Homeowner Rights!

What You Must Do When the Board Turns Your Life Upside Down

Dr. Joyce Starr

The Condo & HOA Defense Kit
Dr. Joyce STARR Publishing
Imprint: Little Guy Pawprint
www.Dr.JoyceStarr.com

Dr. Joyce STARR Publishing
Imprint: Little Guy Pawprint
20533 Biscayne Blvd., Suite 509
Aventura, Florida 33180
www.DrJoyceStarr.com
info@drjoycestarr.com
Phone: 1.786.693.4223

This book is available for special promotions. Contact: info@drjoycestarr.com

First Edition – Published 2007

Printed in the United States and the United Kingdom by Lightning Source.

ISBN13 978-0-9792333-7-1

Library of Congress Control Number 2007903279

Disclaimer

While the publisher and author have used their best efforts in preparing this book, they make no representation or warranties with respect to the accuracy or completeness of the contents of this book and specifically disclaim any implied warranties of merchantability or fitness for a particular purpose. No warranty may be created or extended by sales representatives or written sales materials. The advice and strategies contained herein may not be suitable for your situation. The publisher is not engaged in rendering legal services, and you should consult with an attorney where appropriate. Neither the publisher nor the author shall be liable for any loss of profit or any other commercial damages, including but not limited to special, incidental, consequential or other damages.

The author is not an attorney and does not dispense legal advice. This work is based on public documents and on her personal experiences. The views expressed by the author are solely her opinion.

Dedication

This work is dedicated to the Little Guy for wondrous years of unconditional love, an uncanny talent to make me laugh when all else fails and awe-inspiring leaps into the air from a standstill position – continuous reminder of the utter joy in soaring to new heights. Your presence is daily testament that only a Higher Power could have created such a "purrfect" being.

During the Civil War, General Stonewall Jackson's army found itself on the wrong side of a river. Ordering his engineers to plan and build a bridge, he also told his wagon master that the wagon train must cross the river as soon as possible. Gathering all the logs, rocks and fence rails he could find, the wagon master quickly put together a bridge. As daylight approached, General Jackson was shocked to learn that all the wagons and artillery had crossed the river. "Where are the engineers and what are they doing?" asked Jackson of his wagon master. "They are drawing up plans for a bridge, Sir."

Are you waiting for legislators and agency officials to devise plans to protect your condo and homeowner rights? Or, will you take proactive steps before your rights are placed in jeopardy?

Contents

Acknowledgments

I wish to extend special appreciation to my brother, Robert Starr, Esq., who crafted my defense in a lengthy condo association enforcement battle that few believed could be won – and prevailed against an experienced Florida attorney on his own turf. I also wish to thank his family for selflessly sharing precious family hours.

Warmest appreciation to:

Dr. David I. Goldenberg, a gentleman scholar – for discerning eyes, a special talent for detail and his generosity of spirit;

Wynette Hoffman (BeMusedAuthor.com) – for her dramatic cover design; Polett Villalta (Polett.com) for her art work; and Jonathan D. for story-telling images, artistic guidance and support;

Joanne K., David K., Sylvia M. and Rhoda P. for unwavering support and to those who had the courage to provide witness statements.

I also wish to acknowledge the many dedicated players who have been spearheading the fight for homeowner rights, including:

Florida State Representative Julio Robaino and Jan Bergemann (CCFJ.com) – for their tireless efforts to educate law makers, elected officials, the press and the public.

Sue Bartholomew (OnTheCommons.com) and Evan McKenzie (Privatopia.Blogspot.com) – for giving strong and persistent "voice" to homeowner concerns.

Elizabeth and Arnold McMahon (AHRC.com) – for efforts to stop foreclosures and to attract congressional involvement in this campaign.

"Courage is being scared to death and saddling up anyway."

– John Wayne

"Dear Joyce: I am so very happy that this episode is behind you and your brother. The stress of this case was shattering. Not everyone can stand up to such people. You both have immense inner fortitude. Congratulations on a victory well deserved."

– Family Member

Introduction

My stubborn refusal to submit to frivolous condo association demands is hidden in a cat's tale. However, it could easily have been your story – a Condo or Home Owner Association (HOA) that turned your life upside down over a beloved pet, the color of a mailbox, the size of a fence or minor late payment that mushroomed into a foreclosure.

The names of key players have been masked. In fact, whatever their mistakes or the pain they caused, their identities are no longer relevant. Their actions, by contrast, will resonate as forceful examples of Condo or HOA Boards run amok. It could even happen to them.

This book is written from a dual perspective. While the victim of Board abuse, I also served as a Board member during the entire episode. Self-help strategies offered in this work are steeped in first-hand experiences.

My cat's tale contains an invaluable lesson. When a friend spotted him in a pet-store – "He's your cat!" – I waited several days to visit the shop, hoping he would be sold in the interim. After my first cat passed away, I refused to consider a "replacement."

But I recognized him instantly. A miniature black lion with a perfect face. Huge yellow eyes captured my every move. The store owner explained that he was a show-cat, but his papers had been lost. Even his date of birth was uncertain. "He's your cat," the man declared, echoing my friend's words precisely. "He's your Christmas present." This little ball of fur turned out to be a gift from the universe.

I conferred an ancient Hebraic name, which translates into "Sweet Warrior for Justice." Thereafter, I simply called him the Little Guy. Our first few months together were uneasy. Burmese cats are natural explorers, and they love heights. A virile young male, he assaulted every decorative shelf or object within reach, triumphantly swatting blown glass and beautiful pottery collected during my travels abroad. My floors were strewn with the shards of treasured memories from distant lands. It was not amusing.

My mother departed this world shortly after his arrival, leaving our hearts in shards as well. My father was alone. Making a radical decision, I decided to join him in Florida and continue my international work from that base. Three weeks later, the Little Guy and I arrived at the airport with little time to spare. Passengers were boarding when we reached the gate. Overtaken by thirst, I stopped to buy a soda. Someone bumped my arm, the drink splashed down my blouse and into the cat carry-on bag. We were both a mess. And that's when the gate stewardess declared, "This cat is too large to come on board. He can't stand up in his travel bag. I'm calling security to put him in the luggage compartment."

But before I could lose what remained of my frazzled temper, the Little Guy rose to his full height, hunched his back, and pranced back and forth in less than two feet of space. "Humph!" said the gatekeeper, as she took my ticket. But I was in awe. With pure bravado, he stood up to his adversary and stole my heart.

The Little Guy is now de facto president of his own publishing imprint – Little Guy Pawprint – where he offers homeowners his uniquely empowering message: "Stand up for yourself! Leave them in awe and wonder!"

Defend Your Condo & Homeowner Rights!

Chapter One
Feudal Warlords

Living in a condo or homeowner association is akin to putting a sign on your door declaring, "Nobody is home, and there are diamonds inside." Association members are minority shareholders in multimillion dollar corporations. Yet, few comprehend what their membership entails.

Specifically, condo and homeowner associations are non-profit corporations governed by state laws. They are also the only entities that routinely sue their shareholders, unsuspecting and powerless homeowners, and foreclose on their homes. Fifty-five million Americans reside in communities governed by association documents and rules. Over 1.2 million Floridians reside in condos, and there are over 9,000 HOAs in Arizona alone. The numbers are accelerating across the nation.

Condo and HOAs are run by volunteer Boards of Directors. The typical Board volunteer is well-intentioned but ignorant of proper board practices, the governing rules and state laws. Few have any business training.

Defend Your Condo & Homeowner Rights!

Trouble arises when Board members become commandos. Condo and HOA Board commandos dominate their peers through threats, harassment and frivolous legal sanctions. They persistently attempt to impose their perspectives, priorities and personal agendas on your life.

Some association members regularly disrupt Board meetings, threaten, terrorize and otherwise harm fellow owners or their property. They too are commandos. Such commandos can stimulate Board actions against you. But they cannot authorize the association attorney to take legal steps or force the Board to put a lien on your home. Under certain circumstances, however, they can personally take legal steps against you or place a lien on your home.

Few material possessions are more important than one's home. Yet, millions of Americans are in jeopardy of losing their property in frivolous battles with self-serving, vindictive or unscrupulous Board members.

Owners fail to appreciate how much financial risk is involved. When Board members don't know and don't want to know – and home owners don't know and don't want to know – crimes, including embezzlement, can and do occur.

Defend Your Condo & Homeowner Rights!

The president of a Florida HOA, for example, granted herself sole control over the association's accounts and ATM card *while her fellow board members turned a blind eye.* She embezzled over $500,000 before her crime was uncovered, including $30,000 in repeated withdrawals from an ATM machine at the Seminole Casino and a $5000 withdrawal in a single day.

Police refused to intervene when the woman departed for Pennsylvania, taking the association records with her. "Welcome to association life in Florida, where accountability and enforcement of the law seem to be words unknown!" said Jan Bergemann, president of Cyber Citizens for Justice (CCFJ), a Florida-based group fighting for homeowner rights. According to news reports, the police threatened to arrest anyone who interfered with the woman's moving van. An officer commented: "We hear stories like this all the time, but not with [such] large amounts!"

The association was left with major unpaid bills and the necessity of levying a special assessment to avoid liens on the homes of innocent owners. When a Board member was asked: "Why didn't you read your covenants to better understand your rights and responsibilities," she replied , "I couldn't be bothered with all that legal mumbo jumbo."

7

Defend Your Condo & Homeowner Rights!

When another Board president absconded with insurance funds received for a new roof, owners could do nothing about it. An especially generous and free-wheeling president donated $100,000 of association funds to an outside group fighting for zoning changes in the neighborhood!

As in any corporation, association Board members can be held personally liable for the misuse of funds for personal gain and for taking actions knowingly based on false information, which create financial benefit for themselves or for third parties.

In reality, Board members often operate like feudal warlords, imposing malicious and punitive rules, regulations, and fines. Vexatious lawsuits, harassment and efforts to silence potential whistleblowers – threats against property, lifestyle, positions and pets – have become commonplace.

It's nearly impossible for the typical owner to garner publicity. At the same time, national media exposure can bring an especially outrageous enforcement case to a screeching halt. A soldier's wife living in an HOA was threatened with heavy fines for displaying a "support our troops sign" in her front yard – until the national media came to her rescue.

Defend Your Condo & Homeowner Rights!

Laurie Richter, a Jewish attorney renting a condo in Fort Lauderdale, attracted wide media coverage when the association demanded that she remove a five-inch mezuza from her front doorpost. Sara Liss, a reporter for the prestigious *Jewish Forward*, wrote a lengthy piece about the battle on March 23, 2007, which in turn, attracted the attention of the Anti-Defamation League.

Media exposure, however, can have unintended results. According to the *Jewish Forward*, Richter soon received letters from the association accusing her of "making defamatory comments about the building to the media, leading to a decrease in property values" and threatened to sue her.

My case was highlighted in the *Miami Herald* on two occasions. But this exceptional negative publicity did not bring the board to their knees. Instead, Board members dug even deeper trenches. They even posted the articles on the common bulletin board in the hopes of inciting fellow owners against me.

In the best of worlds, Commandos would be held personally, legally and financially accountable for economic crimes and for capricious legal actions against fellow owners.

Defend Your Condo & Homeowner Rights!

The nation's first Condominium Law Enforcement Pilot Program was launched in Florida in January, 2007. Florida State Representative Julio Robaina created a pilot program with the State Attorney's Office, the Florida Department Of Law Enforcement (FDLE) and the Department of Business and Professional Regulation (DBPR) to train all detectives in Miami/Dade County on "condo crime." After January 2, 2007, callers to the local police no longer received, as I did earlier, the blanket statement that condominium crime is a civil matter.

Instead, the local police will now respond to the report of violations of Florida law. The Miami/Dade pilot program will later be extended into Broward and Palm Beach Counties. Unlike violation letters from the DBPR, if the detectives determine there is probable cause, they will arrest Board members, condominium attorneys, and condominium staff. Owners will not be required to pay for forensic audits. Given probable cause that a criminal violation has been committed, investigators will conduct the necessary forensic audit of condominium records.

Florida State Senator Alex Villalobos and Representative Julio Robaina also sponsored a new homeowner protection bill in February, 2007. Robaina stated: "Without enforcement we have no laws! If a system didn't work for ten or twenty years, don't expect a miracle. We need to change it!"

Defend Your Condo & Homeowner Rights!

Interesting features of the proposed legislation include:

Condominium Associations:

– Notification requirements for planned amendments;

– Detailed regulations for repair after casualty;

– Improved board meetings procedures and elections;

– Improved recall and arbitration procedures;

– Protection against SLAPP suits;

– Stronger disclosure provisions;

– Term limits for board members.

Homeowner Associations:

– Regulation by a government agency with enforcement power;

– Much improved recall provisions and arbitration procedures;

-- Improved provisions protecting finances, budgets and reserve funds;

Defend Your Condo & Homeowner Rights!

– Protection of Constitutional and First Amendment Rights;

– Complete election reform with provisions already successfully used in condos;

-- Stronger disclosure provisions prior to purchase of property.

And for both Condominiums and HOAs:

-- Provisions to allow emotional support animals in associations with pet restrictions;

– A Combined Advisory Council for all associations with equal distribution of Council seats.

In March 2007, Senator Patrick Leahy (Vermont) announced a series of Congressional hearings on the explosion in homeowner foreclosures. Legislative initiatives to protect homeowner rights are also underway in Colorado, North Carolina, Nevada, Pennsylvania, Texas and other states. As these developments unfold, I hope that our Condo and HOA Defense Kit can help homeowners defend their rights, safeguard their investment, protect their health and retain their peace of mind.

Chapter Two
The Abusive Board

In 1938, the name Boston Curtis appeared on the ballot for Committeeman from Wilton, Washington. Boston Curtis was a mule. The town's mayor sponsored the animal to demonstrate that people know very little about their candidates. He proved his point. The mule won!

Abusive Boards behave like stubborn mules – but with less ability, talent or heart for the challenges at hand. They also create unnecessary burdens for others to carry.

There are two kinds of abusive Boards: The entrenched Board and the weak Board. While the entrenched Board exercises too much power, the weak Board exercises too little power. The entrenched Board is comprised of individuals who are re-elected time and again.

Officers can remain in power for decades, with no clear documentation as to how or when they were voted in. Some stories just boggle the mind. In 2006, Residents at the West Garden Village Condominiums filed to recall the board, only to learn that the man they thought was the president wasn't even a board member. In fact, the self-described "leader" of the 64-unit community, hadn't

13

served as president since he was recalled in 1998. His wife replaced him – at least according to the records. He admitted that his wife was president in the past, but neither of them could remember when. Unchastened by the recall action, the brazen "president" declared that he would name his successor when he died.

Secret association elections have been held overseas. A number of owners complain that their Board is primarily or even exclusively comprised of foreign owners and/or owners who do not speak English. In pure contravention of state law, elections are held and plans for the expenditure of funds undertaken when foreign Board members convene or vacation together abroad – literally leaving American owners in the dark.

In McTaggart, et al. v. Burgundy Unit Two Condo. Assoc., Inc. , Case No. 02-5879 (Scheuerman / Final Order / July 18, 2003), the DBPR ruled that:

> "Where the Board members met informally outside the context of formal noticed Board meetings and voted via the device of a written poll whereby each individual Board member who was consulted on a particular matter voted on matters that would come to a vote in a later formal Board meeting, the Board was ordered to

cease its informal meetings and to conduct its meetings in accordance with the statute and documents, with due notice and open to all owners. Board meetings are intended to embrace the discussion of matters coming before the Board for consideration including deliberation and eventual vote, and the association is required to honor the letter and spirit of the law. The Board is a public body that is charged with having its deliberations and decisions made in the sunshine."

Officers were renters, not owners, in several blatant cases. Even so, they were re-elected each year. Fellow owners didn't know where to complain or feared retribution if they did so.

In an article entitled, "The Fight Against Abusive Boards," attorney Jeffrey A. Goldberg (www.condolawyers.com) points out that, "One of the worst situations in the development of community associations is the problem of an abusive Board ... Not every entrenched or weak Board becomes abusive or neglectful of its members. However ... every abusive Board is either weak or entrenched." (This commentary appeared on condolawyers.com.)

Defend Your Condo & Homeowner Rights!

Entrenched Boards, states Goldberg, are less responsive to the needs and desires of association members and devote too much attention towards ensuring their own re-election. They enjoy special powers and perks associated with being in control and exercising power and authority over their neighbors.

By contrast, the weak Board does not have a stable membership. Directors are elected and removed from office with great frequency. Hence, there is little or no "corporate memory" of the association's problems. Bids are rarely announced and contracts seldom signed. The building spirals into decay while Board members focus their energies on getting themselves reelected or fighting with one another. A Board member who created havoc might be recalled one year and re-elected the next because few knew the charges against him and even fewer remember.

Preservation or enhancement of property values is not the primary task of a Board or its directors, despite assertions to the contrary. Economist David I. Goldenberg, (*Creating Home Owner and Condo Association Documents*), explains that:

> "The primarily tasks of those entities are: to operate common ground/property for the benefit of the community; to preserve the

architectural uniformity of the community; and to administer the rules in the governing documents in a cost-effective, prompt and fair manner. Property values depend on many other additional variables far beyond the control of a Board or any combination of its directors. Interest rates are one example. The cost of living in one community as compared another is yet another example. Demand for such housing depends, among other things, on the age distribution of the population and the income/wealth available to each segment of that population."

Board volunteers often lack the experience to run a small kiosk, let alone a multimillion dollar corporation. The typical Board member has little financial or management background. The problem is compounded when Board members who exercised little professional power during prior decades are suddenly granted immense power at your expense. A new Board president exclaimed,"This is so exciting. I never won anything in my life." A Board vice president declared,"I can't believe they voted for me. I've lived here over a decade and hardly speak to anyone."

Abusive Boards and Board members will readily use your money to enhance their prestige and position.

Defend Your Condo & Homeowner Rights!

Their arsenal includes the threat of arbitrary enforcement against unit owners who contest their actions and/or power, as well as selective non-enforcement for unit owners who fall in line. They run up huge legal fees at your expense – creating arbitration and court cases that mire you and your neighbors in months or even years of fruitless stress and strife. "You should have rolled over and played dead," a unit owner told me at the beginning of my condo arbitration nightmare. That's what abusive Boards are counting on: that you will play dead while they pummel your rights and your life.

Abusive Boards create a complex web of invisible personal benefits, including: contractor kickbacks and undocumented home improvements, prime parking spaces and special perks they award to their friends. They declare contract winners without proper bids.

Abusive Boards renovate club houses and lobbies, while allowing your building to crumble. They rely upon the ignorance and/or confusion of fellow Board members and owners to advance their own agendas – spending invaluable resources on personal attacks and petty vendettas. They "selectively enforce" in order to ensure that the masses to see it their way and offer immunity to those who keep them in power.

Defend Your Condo & Homeowner Rights!

Nefarious Board members also encourage chaos behind the scenes, hoping owners will loose track of intractable problems which they created. They whip fellow unit owners into a frenzy while siphoning vital time, energy, common money and happiness to drive their own agenda. They prefer to fix problems with a legal sledge hammer to drive home a point – even if they have to fabricate a conflict to achieve the desired result.

Abusive Boards rely on snitches, cronies, employees and your money to force you to kowtow and comply. As noted above, they also prevaricate, cheat and occasionally steal precious association funds. Abusive Boards also make up rules which end up costing the association thousands and thousands of dollars. It's a bonanza for law firms.

Ironically, homeowners repeatedly elect inexperienced people to the Board for a variety of inane reasons. People vote for a candidate because the person is "nice to me;" "came to my door and asked;" or "drives me to the airport whenever I travel." One of most popular reasons is: "A good friend told me to check the box with his/her name." On occasion, an association member receives the most votes because their last name is first or second on the list. By contrast, naive owners often vote against experienced candidates on equally foolish grounds. One highly qualified Board nominee was told

Defend Your Condo & Homeowner Rights!

by a neighbor, "You're the best candidate on the list. But I won't vote for you because you never wish me a proper good morning on the elevator."

Chapter Three
Association Warfare

I dealt with international conflicts throughout my professional career. I've run through barrages of bullets, sought cover during bombings and been helicoptered out of war zones. But nothing prepared me for association warfare in Florida. Abusive Boards destroy their victims with painful legal calibration.

Your immediate reaction may well be: If I keep my head down and remain invisible, they will not bother me. The majority of homeowners lust for "the good life" so badly that they willingly absorb repeated blows from abusive Board members to retain this delusion. But invisible is not invincible.

Advertised as care-free living, the condo and HOA reality is seldom as blissful as developers and Boards would like us to believe. When personal agendas and arrogance take precedence over sound judgment, carefree is easily transformed into an enduring nightmare for unwitting unit owners. When abusive Board power is unleashed in frivolous legal adventures, the toxic result is litigation heaven for specialized association attorneys.

Defend Your Condo & Homeowner Rights!

Condo and HOA enforcement cases have spiraled out of control. Foreclosures and loss of homes resulting from an initial failure to pay a minor fee or fine – which then escalated into massive overdue payments – have taken on epidemic proportions. The financial vulnerability and health threat is enormous.

Journalist Willowdean Vance stated in a commentary on the AHRC website, "Any hearing on foreclosure scams will fail unless we reveal the connection to ... deaths from stress related heart attacks and strokes caused by racketeering law firms lining their pockets with foreclosure profits."

A drawn out legal action can quickly run up fees equivalent to a hefty payment on a new home. And these figures do not include the drain on association coffers when enforcement cases are declared moot. Your association foots the bill with your money. Our Board spent over $25,000 in legal fees in their war against my pet cat, along with an additional $5,000 battling against two other units owners in a vain attempt to bolster their case against us. We won and the other two were declared moot. Thirty thousand dollars went down the proverbial legal drain.

In my condo battle, the association attorney pressed on with the case even when he knew there was a high probability that the association would lose. In principle, the association attorney should first determine if the case is valid and probably winnable. Many do so. In our situation, the attorney failed to ascertain whether the Board had the authority to pursue the case, whether pets were owned by former and current Board members and whether my cat resided in my home beyond the statute of limitations!

Why would an attorney risk losing a case? The attorney who transforms Board wishes into billable hours does not want to lose a case. But failing to win is not a failure for the attorney. Win or lose, the attorney brings money into the law firm, and there is also no public database listing his/her track record in association cases. The attorney can also blame the client for failing to disclose all relevant facts.

Owners pray that justice will prevail. But prayers are a weak shield against a determined Board. Enforcement cases are seldom won on the merits of the case. They're won on the ability to finance costly and protracted procedures. Condo and HOA attorneys file repeated motions to bleed their victim's dry, often forcing owners to concede to unreasonable settlements. Many a case was settled for monetary reasons. Most often, it is just too costly to fight.

Defend Your Condo & Homeowner Rights!

The legal warfare strategy can be characterized as "kill the owner with his/her money." A condo enforcement action over two pet dogs incurred over $140,000 in legal fees for the owner. A member of an HOA was fined $3,000 for failing to clean her roof when demanded. A minor balcony dispute left the homeowner $70,000 in the red. Enforcement action over a $2,500 fence went to the Florida Supreme Court. It cost the association $360,000 in legal fees when they lost and also resulted in a Special Assessment for the owners. Disagreement over a brown patch of grass escalated into a $300,000 legal bill for the HOA member.

Association members pay a heavy price for frivolous legal adventures by their Board – both in terms of misspent funds and misspent attention to urgent priorities. According to Dr. Goldenberg, opponents of oppressive Boards only have a few effective options at this time. These include:

1. Suffer in Silence;
2. Relocate Elsewhere;
3. Modify your Governing Documents;
4. Pray for Legislative Intervention
5. Recall the Board;
6. Sue the Board.

You might also pray that your legislature will solve the problem – or for other forms of Divine Intervention –

so long as you're operating on the Lord's schedule. Suitable revisions to your governing documents should offer more rapid resolution. In reality, modifying governing documents is akin to mounting a multi-year expedition to the antarctic – requiring immense technical knowledge and fortitude.

Dr. Goldenberg stresses that recalling the Board only makes sense if all three of the following conditions can be met. First, competent people must be available and willing to serve on the Board. Second, the newly installed Board members must have enough votes to control the Board. Third, the new Board must revise the governing documents to preclude troublesome practices in the future.

Even so, a recall may be ineffective. Owners who succeed in recalling board members may not be able to remove them. Florida Boards have five business days to challenge a recall. Boards have also been known to ignore a recall vote and continued with business as usual. The distraught homeowners were deserted at the altar by the Arbitration Bureau. There was no further recourse.

Suing the Board, as discussed above, is a costly enterprise. According to Dr. Goldenberg, suits can prove cost-effective only under a rare combination of circumstances: one has a very strong case, along with immense   patience and persistence;   and there are enormous damages to collect from sufficiently wealthy defendants or insurers.

Chapter Four
Abuse of Your Funds

Owners who sue their Boards seldom win. This is especially true where an alleged misuse of funds is alleged. Contrary to homeowner expectations, their state arbitration agency – if there is one – will likely hide behind a variety of excuses to avoid intervention in financial matters.

Florida's Arbitration Bureau (the DBPR), for example, ruled in case after case over the last decade that the Arbitrator could not involve himself in the question when "a condominium's declaration vests discretion in the Board of directors and disputes [involve] the alleged breach of fiduciary duty by one or more members of the Board." (Migliorino v. The Jupiter Beachcomber Condo. Assoc. Inc., Case No. 2003-06-0842 (Mnookin / Final Order Dismissing Petition for Arbitration / June 3, 2003.)

The unit owner in this case claimed that the association improperly paid for the repair of two limited common element patios, which would result in a higher assessment charged to the unit owner. The petition for arbitration was dismissed for lack of jurisdiction over the levy of a fee or assessment. The ruling stated:

27

"Pursuant to section 718.1255 F.S., disputes eligible for arbitration do not include those involving the levy of a fee or assessment. Furthermore, if the unit owner were to allege that the association misused its funds by paying for the patio repairs, the arbitration division would still lack jurisdiction to entertain the claim because it involves a breach of fiduciary duty on the part of the association. Disputes involving the alleged breach of fiduciary duty by one or more directors are also not within the jurisdiction of the Arbitrator."

When are directors personally responsible for their conduct as directors? A violation of the condominium act must be done 'willfully and knowingly.' According to an online article by Florida attorney Michael E. Rehr (www.rehrlaw.com): "No recourse may be had against Board members personally" where simple negligence is involved. His analysis holds the key to the dilemma facing homeowners.

"I am often called by a disgruntled condominium unit owner and asked to file a lawsuit against the individual members of the Board of directors of the condominium association for what the owner considers some type of wrongful conduct. A common situation is when a Board doesn't pay certain bills and is sued by a vendor, resulting in an obligation to pay not only the debt, but also the vendor's substantial legal fees...Another situation is when an association President enters into a contract that the owner considers very one-sided for a vendor, or at a price that is too high.

"Section 718.303 of the Condominium Act provides that: 'Actions for damages ... for failure to comply with these provisions (i.e, the provisions of the Act), may be brought by the association or by a unit owner against: ... (d) any director who willfully and knowingly fails to comply with these provisions.' A similar provision of the Florida Not-for-Profit Act, Section 617.0834, may apply and provides for immunity from personal liability unless the director's actions constitute a criminal violation, or provided an improper personal benefit to the director, or was reckless, committed in bad faith or with malicious purpose. Thus, from the applicable statutes the Courts have concluded: 'association directors are immune from liability in their individual capacity, absent fraud, criminal activity or self-dealing/unjust enrichment.' A violation of the condominium

act must be done 'willfully and knowingly.'
More than simple negligence is required before
personal liability for monetary damages may be
imposed...[In] a case where a director breached
his fiduciary duty by failing to renew fire
insurance on the association's clubhouse, the
individual director was not held personally
liable for his negligence even though his actions
were clearly wrong. In another case where the
Board members failed to properly administer
insurance proceeds from Hurricane Andrew,
the Board members were not personally liable
because there was no fraud or crime committed
and the Board members did not derive any
person benefit from their conduct, even though
they may have been negligent."
(http://www.rehrlaw.com/when_are_director
s_personally_liable.htm)

Some states do a much better job than others in
protecting owner rights.   In Illinois, for example,
directors have a fiduciary duty to comply with specific
requirements in the declaration. Illinois attorney
Marshall N. Dickler (www.dicklerlaw.com) wrote:

"If the Board members fail to comply with the
clear declaration requirements, they can be held
in breach of their fiduciary duty. This principal

was stated in a case dealing with an association's alleged failure to proceed in accordance with the first purchase option requirements in the declaration. Illinois law requires that directors cannot do anything that would interfere with the ability of the association to accomplish its purpose. Doing anything which interferes with the association's ability to accomplish its purpose is a violation of the directors' obligations as a matter of law. This principal was set forth in a case where the developer Board did not adequately reserve on behalf of the association." (http://www.dicklerlaw.com/news_responsibl e.htm)

The 2007 investigative project initiated by Florida legislator Julio Robaina and the Florida District Attorney's office (see Chapter One) will hopefully empower Florida homeowners who reside in "trial" areas to take more aggressive legal steps against criminal actions by individual Board members.

Naive residents are often in good company with state legislators. According to Robaina, associations are represented by influential law firms that have the money, unity and clout to keep state and national legislators in a fog about condo Board abuse.

Defend Your Condo & Homeowner Rights!

"Legislators are up against a powerful group of law firms that want to retain control. They claim that we (those with opposing views) are a bunch of idiots," said Robaina. Association attorneys are often the only ones who walk away with money – which is why they can afford an ear in the capital, a voice in the law, and handsome payments for lobbyists to fight against homeowner rights."

Dr. Wayne T. Moses, president of the Humanitarian Society, questioned whether homeowner associations are a good place to come home to. His June 26, 2006 *Sun- Sentinel* commentary is excerpted below:

> "Service providers such as management companies and attorneys [realize] that these associations are a great cash cow. The reason: Legislators all around the nation created laws governing HOAs – ambiguous laws, easy to interpret any which way you want to twist them and nearly unenforceable. This opens the door for all kinds of shenanigans – from just plain power-hungry board members to greedy managers and attorneys. The money is always there, and don't forget, your home is collateral for any bills they create.

Defend Your Condo & Homeowner Rights!

"Our property values will not go up because we all have the same beige-colored doors ... the same peach-colored shingles, [or] flowers with bright colors in the front yards ... Better times will only return if we ... create the laws that will stop most of these shenanigans."

"Always forgive your enemies - nothing
annoys them so much."

– Oscar Wilde

Chapter Five
Good Life Turns Grim

People often asked, "Why risk so much for a cat?"

As my neighbor declared: "This battle is not about a four-legged animal. It's really about a two-legged creature." There was no pet "problem" in our building until I raised a red flag over toxic mold in our corridors and questioned Board management practices.

When my condo saga began, I was looking forward to a freshly painted apartment and new professional arenas. A film treatment was in progress, along with a book. Instead, I became embroiled in a two-year struggle over mold, money and pets, with my home as the battleground.

My parents moved into our condo when the building was first constructed. My mother was prescient, and my father wisely trusted her instincts. She chose a condo with an exhilarating view of the sea in a sweet, medium-rise building. The building stands at the gateway to a small city which today has only about 500,000 inhabitants and offers one of the highest ratios of trees per capita.

Defend Your Condo & Homeowner Rights!

In 2003, dad left the condo in my care. By the third week of January, 2004, I was steeped in the final phase of renovation, with little respite besides my morning swim and visits to the local cinema. I wrote to a friend, "I want to create a space that will lift the spirits of those who enter. I care about this condominium, have treasured memories and am happy here."

My parents served on the Board consecutively for almost 20 years. Both served as treasurer for lengthy periods. I knew many neighbors. Several encouraged me to run for the Board. On the one hand, I wanted absolutely nothing to do with politics – condo or otherwise. I was determined to leave the "political" phase of my life behind. Yet, I asked myself: Is this a responsible point of view? Doesn't one have a responsibility to play a civic role? My brother and father encouraged me to get involved.

On January 25, 2005, I was elected to the Board of Directors. Little did I suspect that my personal dreams would soon be transformed into a two-year nightmare. The following week, my painting contractor alerted me to the presence of mold on the corridor ceiling outside my unit. Aware of the potential health consequences of mold, I was concerned. I immediately phoned the president. She, in turn, phoned the property manager.

Defend Your Condo & Homeowner Rights!

We had a heated exchange. The manager insisted that the discoloration on the corridor ceilings were merely harmless dirt. He directed the building's engineer and maintenance employees to clean the area with Clorox and paint over it. I feared for their safety. Direct exposure to airborne mold, without proper equipment, can be dangerous.

I hit my first wall as a new Board member. Calling attention to a possible health emergency, I was ignored by the property manager and by the Board president. The president said she was busy with more pressing matters and had no further time to discuss it.

I rarely recall my dreams, much less commit them to paper. But the evening of the mold encounter, I dreamt that my father and I went to see a movie. His view was not as good as mine, so I took his seat instead. Indeed, I would soon take over his "seat" by becoming a whistleblower against the same property manager my fathered motioned to dismiss over decade earlier. The manager was rehired after dad left the Board.

A restrictive pet clause in our condo Declaration was effectively ignored for over thirty years ("failure to enforce"). Numerous owners openly kept pets in their units, including prior and current members of the Board. There was no doubt in my mind or anyone else for that matter that this Condo Commando attack was really about a whistleblower – a Board member who raised thorny issues – and not about a cat.

Sacrificing a beloved higher pet soul in the hopes of assuaging a group of mean-spirited condo Board officers who didn't deserve to kiss his tiny paws was simply not an action that I was willing to entertain.

A year into the struggle, I told our association president that her refusal to remediate toxic mold was ultimately between her and God. She responded: "I don't believe in God."

Chapter Six
The Whistleblower

How do you become a candidate for Condo or HOA enforcement? It's far easier than you think. Here are some steps you can take:

- ♦ Agitate over meaningless issues;
- ♦ Agitate over serious issues;
- ♦ Annoy neighbors as much as possible;
- ♦ Become a whistleblower;
- ♦ Demand to see public records;
- ♦ Hide a pet in no-pet building;
- ♦ Refuse to respond to warning letters;
- ♦ Raise probing questions at Board meetings;
- ♦ Refuse to read your documents or rules;
- ♦ Violate association documents and rules.

Additional Qualifications: 1) You can't afford to hire an attorney or 2) You can afford to hire several attorneys but don't stand a chance of winning your case.

Like most bullies, abusive association Board members usually choose their targets wisely. They often pursue homeowners who lack the financial means and/or ability to defend themselves and are more likely to cave in than bear the costs of a struggle. The whistleblower is a doubly valuable target. Legal action against the whistleblower is a premeditated warning to other owners who might be willing to contest "business as usual." The whistleblower who complains about failure of maintenance is a perfect candidate.

A terrified whistleblower wrote to the Florida Ombudsman for advice when he was sued for libel and harassment by his Board.

> "I am being taken to court by my Board of directors for harassment and libel. They say that the information I gave to the membership on the hiring of a non- licensed contractor, no insurance, no workmen's compensation and not pulling permits is untrue. Yet the city building inspectors and the detective found this to be true and put a stop work order on the front door, while the contractor was fined and almost put in jail. They say that their reputation was damaged and this was also considered harassment."

Generally, one cannot be sued for statements about the public activities of a public figure such as Board members. But a public figure with deep pockets can always find an attorney willing to initiate or threaten such action. The association has little chance of winning, but the homeowner is forced to hire an attorney. The Ombudsman cautioned:

"Your condominium documents should state whether mediation or arbitration is required prior to initiating litigation. Meanwhile, if you have been named as a Defendant in a lawsuit and served with a Summons and Complaint, then you should retain the services of an attorney to represent and protect your interests."

Collateral damage is often far-reaching. Your physical property, family and/or friends can be affected. Karoline Kuebler, a HOA member in North Carolina who works on behalf of disenfranchised homeowners, wrote:

"Whistleblowers suffer harassment, threats, retaliation and property damages. It is not just one person whom they attack. They go after the entire family and even friends in many instances. Whistleblowers in condos and HOAs should be protected by the Whistleblower Act."

Defend Your Condo & Homeowner Rights!

An especially clever whistleblower caught her property manager on video tape pouring a chemical into her window. Homeowners have even alleged that their lawns were poisoned to force "beautification" of their property. A homeowner who left Christmas lights up beyond the holiday season was accused of threatening airline flight patterns and witchcraft!

My personal struggle over toxic mold illustrates what many encounter when raising uncomfortable questions about pressing maintenance matters. It could just as easily be your story. Mold spores are airborne. A State of Florida Health Inspector confirmed that mold spores were spawning outside my door, blackening the common area corridor ceiling and ceilings throughout the building.

Condominium owners have an obligation to remediate mold in their units. But how can they protect themselves against mold spores that fly into their unit every time they open their door? They can't! As I soon found out, homeowners are virtually powerless to force a condo Board president and Board supporters with a different "agenda" to remediate toxic mold.

My multi-year mold saga was finally revealed by Ana Veciana-Suarez of the *Miami Herald* on October 10, 2005. She wrote:

Defend Your Condo & Homeowner Rights!

"Joyce Starr first noticed the mold on her condominium corridor's ceilings in February 2004, when a contractor pointed it out ... She immediately notified [the] Board president, who, in turn, told the property manager. But almost 20 months, several reports and a flurry of letters and accusations later, the mold is still snaking its way along the corridors.

"By November 2004, the Board had received an engineering report documenting the water damage and the spread of the fungus. The report also recommended that experienced mold remediators be hired. Getting bids for the removal work took several more months. [The president] says the magnitude of the job and differing opinions on how to do it slowed the process.

"But Starr doesn't buy that. She claims that [the president] has delayed working on the mold remediation because [she] wants to fold in a special assessment for balcony renovation with the assessment for the mold. The balcony expense is about $1 million, the mold about $250,000. 'It's a matter of bookkeeping,' [the president] says. 'We don't want different assessments. It's easier that way.' Frustrated,

Starr brought in a health inspector to do a walk-through and contacted the state condo ombudsman, the Aventura police and State Rep. Julio Robaina.

"This past June, she also testified before the Governor's Advisory Council on Condominiums, questioning the accountability and practices of her condo Board. The mold is still there. 'A year and a half has gone by since the mold was first detected,' she told the council. 'If and when action is finally taken, I fear that the mold remediation will be done shoddily.' "

According to Florida law, condo associations must address maintenance issues in "a reasonable amount of time." But there is no definition of reasonable and no state agency has the responsibility or power to force your condo Board to remediate mold.

As you read above, our Board president assured the *Miami Herald* that remediation steps were in progress. A month later – on November 2, 2005 – we had another Board battle over mold. Our president declared that night: "I have no health concerns about the mold. We should remove it. But I am not the least bit worried that it will make anyone sick." A Board

44

member leading the offensive against comprehensive mold remediation told unit owners: "The only way mold in this building can make you sick is if you lick it off the walls." He then went on to use/abuse Environmental Protection Agency (EPA) and Harvard website materials in support of this outrageous claim.

Association members attending the meeting were up in arms, demanding that remediation begin as soon as possible. By that point, there was almost total agreement among the owners that the corridor ceilings, walls and common areas were mold toxic.

Engineering experts contracted by our Board stated unequivocally that this mold must removed by professionally certified mold remediation specialists using sophisticated EPA-approved procedures and protective equipment. Yet, on December 11, 2005, I noticed debris on our corridor floor. When I looked up to determine the source, I was dumbstruck by what I saw: a 4 inch hole in the corridor ceiling. The Board previously approved the installation of smoke prevention doors on each floor. Slicing into our ceilings was apparently part of the work plan.

I asked our Board president why she allowed this work to proceed prior to mold remediation. Her reply was eerily reminiscent of our first discussion about mold in

Defend Your Condo & Homeowner Rights!

February 2004: "I don't know anything about it. I guess it is part of what they have to do. I'm busy now and can't do anything about it."

I insisted that she instruct the company to close the holes immediately and to clean up the debris. She replied, "I'm sure they will get around to it." I told her that mold spores in our ceiling ducts were surely flying through those holes as we spoke and asked: "Do you think that mold spores cower in a little corner of the ceiling, awaiting a special invitation to enter the corridor?" She said she didn't know.

I phoned the State of Florida Health Department. I knew that the Department had no statutory authority over mold in condominiums. But the person in charge of indoor air quality might provide a telephone number I could call. He was on vacation. I next phoned the Department of Environmental Resource Management (DERM) of Dade-Miami County, only to be informed that DERM's statutory authority is limited to outdoor air quality matters.

I contacted the director of the building division of our city, who explained that the category "environment" is not included in the Florida building code and that the Building Code does not recognize the mold issue! While the Florida Building Code contains reference to water damage, it does not address mold that develops from water damage in common areas. The director said he receives many complaints from distraught condominium owners about toxic mold in condominium common areas, but was powerless to take enforcement action. One high-level government official conveyed his personal frustration at the lack of an effective "address" in such cases. He frankly admitted that there was no one I could turn to. Under present Florida law (or lack thereof), condo directors and condo property managers cannot be held legally responsible for "failure of mold remediation."

Where is the Governor? Where are our legislators? Where is the Environmental Protection Agency? As of the writing of this book, no government official or department had yet lifted a hand to assist Florida condo owners helplessly exposed to mold in corridors and common areas. By the close of 2006, thirty-four months after I raised the first warning, the Board failed to approve, let alone proceed with, a contract for mold remediation. The request for bids was issued anew in February 2007, when the new property manager and a new Board started from ground zero.

"This is the closest I can imagine to living under the Gestapo or the Inquisition. They have the same horrible power over our lives. There is no justice for the so-called unit owner – and no one to speak to. "

– Distraught Condo Owner

Chapter Seven
The Agitator

Agitators are often feared, loathed and shunned by their neighbors. I was an agitator, Board victim and Board member. In my months on the Board, I raised the alarm about mold, questioned the Board's procedures and failure of fiduciary responsibility, alerted the Florida Ombudsman to illegal Board practices, spoke out at the Governor's Advisory Council on Condominiums meeting in June 2005 and went to the police in July 2006 about the failure to remediate mold.

In early 2006, I discovered that our president and property manager had failed to file insurance claims with both our insurance company and FEMA after Hurricane Wilma in late 2005. She advised the insurance company that we would not meet our deductible. This "mistake" would have denied the association over a million dollars in reimbursable funds. I drafted a detailed memo (see below) to owners and personally delivered it to the 144 units in our building.

Defend Your Condo & Homeowner Rights!

"ATTENTION UNIT OWNERS

"From: Dr. Joyce Starr, Member of the Board, 1/18/2006

"1. **Hurricane Damage:** As you are aware, our association did not file insurance claims for damages incurred during hurricane Wilma. Our Board president repeatedly stated that there was no reason to file because we would not make the deductible. This did not make sense to me. In my capacity as a member of the Board, I contacted our insurance agent, insurance company and the hurricane insurance adjuster assigned to our condominium.

"I learned that our insurance agent automatically filed for hurricane damage on behalf of all clients following Hurricane Wilma, including our association. The insurance company then assigned an adjuster to work with each condominium. The adjuster contacted our property manager and Board president. Soon thereafter he visited our building. During that visit, our president presented a list of damages demonstrating that we will not meet the $250,000 hurricane deductible. This list was not presented to Members of the Board or shared with unit owners.

"2. **Estimates**: The insurance adjuster asked for more detailed estimates on all damages. Four months have passed, but estimates were not submitted. Hurricane damage is considered "catastrophic," and thus cannot be used against us to raise our premium.

"3. **FEMA**: I also learned that our association is eligible for hurricane disaster relief from FEMA and/or from the Small Business Administration (SBA), including possible grant assistance from FEMA and/or a low interest rate loan through the SBA. But no paperwork was submitted.

"4. **Assessment Estimate**: Potential insurance coverage and FEMA/SBA hurricane assistance were not factored into the $1.3 million Special Assessment estimate. Why are the president and property manager so anxious to borrow $1.3 million, without exploring every possible option to reduce this burden? Your vote in the coming election is critical. We must remove the property manager and put an end to the president's disregard for unit owner rights, including the right to be kept fully informed. Relieved of duties by several condos in the near vicinity, the property manager should not play a role in our association's loan."

Defend Your Condo & Homeowner Rights!

Our president was forced to admit her glaring "mistake." Insurance claims were filed soon thereafter. However, as no good deed goes unpunished, I was defeated for reelection to the Board the following week.

Several owners told me, "You're one of the most qualified people in the building, but why were you so **aggressive** on the insurance issue?"

I tried to explain what over a million dollars could mean for each unit on a prorated basis. Most were unmoved. The more compelling issue was that their friend – a person who joins them for dinners, shows and card games – was embarrassed.

Moreover, thirty-eight unit owners were not living in their condos at the time of the new election. Little or no effort was undertaken to compare signatures on the outer envelope with those on file in the association office.

As reported by Valmore Lucier, author of *Condo Board Election Revolt*, Board members and property mangers have been known to remove ballots from their envelopes, replace them with pre-checked ballots, reseal the envelope and sign it on the outside. In this instance, owners were directed to mail their ballots directly to the property manager, rather than to the association office.

The very person who lit the match for enforcement action against our family was now counting the votes for and against. He also warned the Board in mid-February 2006 that they could be sued by owners if they drop the case!

Dismissed by my father and his fellow Board members in the late 1990s, this man was thereafter rehired and allowed to dominate our association for another decade. Subsequent Boards members blithely approved almost all of his recommendations. Yet, we were facing a massive assessment and substantial increases in our monthly maintenance fees due in large part to the failure to properly maintain the building in the intervening years.

Fortunately, the property manager was now the one under fire. His stranglehold on the building was about to go up in smoke. Delving into public records, a curious unit owner discovered that the manager had been "relieved of his duties" by a number associations in the area. Calls were made and data collected. The folder of potentially embarrassing information was growing thicker by the day.

The rapidly deteriorating state of the building was increasingly obvious to the residents. By now, black mold traversed large areas of our common area corridor ceilings. One elderly owner told me, "I never looked up before, so I never saw it." While no direct connection can be established, others suffered from frequent colds, sore throats and allergic reactions.

It was also learned that the association attorney was an officer in one of the property manager's companies. While not illegal or unethical, it raised certain questions about conflict of interest regarding our case. The property manager had scores to settle against our family, which could potentially deliver large legal fees to the attorney. In condo corporation heaven, such information should have been revealed by both parties at the very start of the enforcement action, quickly putting such concerns to rest.

The straw that apparently triggered the property manager's departure was the revelation, as reported in my memo, that he was relieved of duties by other condominiums. On the eve of the election, the president announced that our property manager submitted his resignation earlier that day and she accepted it. He was gone forever. I felt like Dorothy in *The Wizard of Oz.*

The new Board voted to move from part-time management a few hours a week to a full-time property manager as of March 1, 2006. At one point in the meeting, an owner stood up and said, "Although I am happy to see some new faces on the Board, I have never experienced a nastier group of Board members. You should attend classes to learn how to behave." This homeowner wasn't addressing anyone in particular.

The president piped up, "Thank you very much for calling me nasty."

Another owner then declared: "The Board vice president has served for almost a decade, while three of you served for the past half decade. You've let this building reach its lowest point. You should be ashamed."

A third resident said, "This building could not get any lower. Under your administration, there is nothing that works as it should."

The property manager hired a few weeks later proved to be professional, diligent and caring. He took a methodical and "above board" approach to the challenges facing our small community. Such superior service was long overdue at the Good Life Condominium.

Defend Your Condo & Homeowner Rights!

What steps can you take to report suspected failures of maintenance, breaches of fiduciary responsibility, possible misuse of funds, violations of rules and procedures or related association problems?

Start a paper trail. Send a certified return-receipt letter to your Board of Directors and/or to the registered agent of the association. Describe the problem and its location. Request a response within thirty days.

If the Board fails to reply, you can sue to force the association into action. In 2006, owners at the Bay Winds Community Association in Palm Beach County, Florida, sued their association, individual Board members and the association attorney for "Violation of the Plaintiffs Constitutionally protected rights as provide by Article I §§2.4.5; Violation of Florida State §720.304; Violation of Florida State §720.303; Violation of Florida Statute §720. 306(1)(c); Breach of Fiduciary Duty; Breach of Implied Covenant of Good Faith and Fair Dealing; Fraud and Civil Conspiracy."

Unfortunately, taking legal action against your association is also the easiest way to sue yourself. The Board must direct the association attorney to respond, and legal fees are incurred. If the association prevails, you will be held responsible for reimbursement of those fees. Before taking the legal path, assess all options and consequences, as well as possible costs. One association sued five Board members who embezzled money. The association won but couldn't collect a dime, since the Board members quickly declared bankruptcy!

You can also file a complaint with your state condo or HOA ombudsman or through the state agency that regulates condo and homeowner associations. In Florida, for example, owners can contact the Ombudsman at 850-922-7671 or file a complaint with the Dept. of Business and Professional Regulation: www.myflorida.com/dbpr/lsccondominiums/formsco mplaint.pdf. Write to the DBPR at: 1940 N. Monroe St., Tallahassee, FL, 32399, attn: Division of Land Sales, Condominiums and Mobile Homes. Alternatively, Florida residents can write to State Representative Julio Robaina at: julio.robaina@myfloridahouse.gov or at his office: 6741 SW 24th St., Suite 19, Miami, FL, 33155. He played a key role in helping pass a law creating the Florida Condo Ombudsman and the Condominium Advisory Council.

After considerable research, *Miami Herald* reporter Ana Veciana-Suarez discovered that neither the Florida Ombudsman nor the Florida Department of Business and Professional Regulation have enforcement power. In the end, she wrote, "Be prepared for a drawn-out process that may have no resolution."

"Worry is a thin stream of fear trickling through the mind. If encouraged, it cuts a channel into which all other thoughts are drained. "

– Arthur S. Roche

Chapter Eight
How to Respond to
Warning Letters

In the first week of October 2004, I received an envelope from the company that provided management services for our condominium. It contained an unsigned letter on Board stationary from the "Board of Directors."

This warning letter contained a demand that my pet cat be removed within thirty days. As a current Board member, I knew the board had neither formally discussed nor voted on this matter. Moreover, the document falsely stated: "We are not aware of any other animals at the building."

Board members were aware that pet cats and parakeets had been kept in the building over many decades, including by prior Board officers. Moreover, I was personally aware that a former Board president who still served as a Board officer had been housing his girlfriend's dog each weekend for several years. The letter purported to be authorized by the Board. Were my fellow Board members aware of the letter? A colleague informed me that he had not been privy to any such Board discussion.

Defend Your Condo & Homeowner Rights!

I showed the letter to two former long-standing Board members of stature. Both approached the president and insisted that the frivolous action be dropped. She refused. I approached her as well. She told me: "They say I am a weak president. Well, I will prove to you and everyone else that I am a strong president."

I reminded her that we made no effort to conceal the presence of my cat; that the Little Guy was well known to building staff, neighbors and to Board members. Any enforcement action in such circumstances would contravene well-settled practices of many decades.

Determined to use this case to assert her personal authority, our Board president would not be deterred by those facts.

The letter I received stated:

"Dear Ms. Starr:

"It has come to our attention that you have a cat living with you. As you know, this is against the rules and regulations of the Condominium Assoc.

"We must enforce this Rule and are giving you 30 days to have the animal removed or it will be necessary to take legal action to resolve this matter. We appreciate the fact that you are attached to your animal. We are not aware of any other animals in the building. If you know of any, please inform us so we write a similar letter.

"Sincerely,

"Board of Directors"

If the Board sends you a warning letter, there are concrete steps you can take, as discussed further below. But first, there are a number of " human" reactions you must avoid and/or bring under control.

If you receive a warning letter, DO NOT:

> * Panic.
>
> * Tear up the letter away or put it in your cat's kitty litter.
>
> * Scribble epithets and place the letter under the president's door.
>
> * Assume that you or your friends can reason with the president or other Board officers and change his/her/their collective minds.

Defend Your Condo & Homeowner Rights!

* Presume that a single conversation with the president or any other officer is a substitute for putting your intentions in writing. It's not!

* Storm into the association office, slam the door, throw the letter on the desk and tell the president you plan to sue her/him.

* Physically threaten or swear at any Board member.

* Give the Board a list of other violators. You're a victim, not a snitch. You will also need the help of those people in the near future.

* Call television stations or newspapers. You're only in the first phase of enforcement. Without sound research and facts, your case has no media value or interest.

* Contact the association attorney for advice or comment. Such a call places the attorney in conflict of interest situation, which he must ethically avoid or resolve in favor of his client, the association. The association pays his fees. Although you indirectly pay a portion of those fees, the attorney represents the entire membership and not the individual homeowner.

Defend Your Condo & Homeowner Rights!

<u>Here is a list of proactive steps that you must take if you receive a warning letter</u>:

Read Your Documents: The letter should give you thirty days to reply. Before responding, determine if you are in fact in violation. Read your documents, bylaws and rules very carefully. If the issue is still unclear, consult with an attorney who is well-versed in condo or HOA laws in your state.

Attorneys normally charge about $200 - $225 an hour for this type of work. Case review and preparation of your response to the association warning letter could take several billable hours. The question is: Can you afford this service? If not, you must take the time to read the documents yourself.   But what if the documents go on for hundreds of pages? How do you find the correct passage?

Identify Relevant Text. The warning letter should stipulate or refer to the particular section or passage. If no text is cited, politely ask the association president or property manager to refer you to the rule(s) in question. Do so in writing. Alternatively, if your president and/or manager is willing, record the conversation on audio, video or digital tape. Remember, you must ask and receive permission to make such a recording.

Defend Your Condo & Homeowner Rights!

Keep Accurate Records. Maintain complete records of your letters and conversations about the warning letter – including the date, time and what was said.

Know What You Owe. Enforcement cases often take root over insignificant sums of money (a few hundred dollars or less), which the owner unwittingly failed to pay or felt they should not be required to pay. The enforcement action might even be groundless. A member of our condo received a late fee warning for an assessment payment made three years prior. If you cannot locate financial records, you cannot prove what you owe or paid.

Respond to Warnings. A combination of ballooning late fees and legal fees can rapidly result in the loss of a home. In numerous instances, the owner could not afford to make the change or to pay the money due. Rather than attempt to negotiate a reasonable response time and/or payment schedule, they ignored repeated warnings. In 2006, a young mother with three young children was forced out of her home over $262 that her estranged husband still owed the HOA. Two sheriff's deputies, a crew of movers and the management representative emptied out the house and left the family's possessions at the curb. Her two-year old daughter and sons, ages five and eighty, were traumatized. "There was no compassion for my kids," she told the press. The association returned possession of the home when it received payment from the husband, but the woman vowed that she would never return. "I cannot get over the hurt my children are feeling."

If you're in violation and owe money, take the following actions:

Determine What You Owe. It's imperative that you inquire in writing – and receive a response – regarding the exact sum owed to the penny. When confident about the number, write to the president detailing what you intend to do. If you can pay, include a check for the full amount – including interest, penalties and legal fees. Be sure to state that a check for the full amount is enclosed! Copy your letter to each Board member and to the property manager. Request confirmation that all financial obligations, fines, fees, and bills have now been met in full. If you do not receive confirmation, write to the president once again and reiterate your demand. Attach a copy of your check and your original letter.

At Minimum, Make a Partial Payment. If you cannot pay the full amount, make a partial payment and propose a reasonable payment schedule for the rest. Request confirmation that your proposal is accepted.

Make the Requested Change. Make the change requested within the thirty-day window or advise the Board in writing when you intend to make the change.

Certify Your Mail. Send all letters by certified mail, with a return receipt requested. When you write to the president, copy all Board Directors and the property manager by certified mail as well. Letters to the president and to Board members should be sent directly to the association office. Do not mail letters to their homes.

Copy the Association Attorney. If the association attorney is already involved in your case, copy the attorney on your letter(s). Moreover, you also should write a letter directly to the attorney, requesting confirmation that all outstanding obligations have been met in full. Under no circumstances should you tell the attorney "what you really think." Send the letter before half of your allotted time has elapsed, giving the certified letter sufficient days to arrive. I sent a certified letter to our association attorney from a post office that was down the street from his office. Over ten days elapsed before anyone signed for the letter. This may not have been intentional. Certified mail is often slower than regular mail.

Defend Your Condo & Homeowner Rights!

Do Not Rely on Certified Mail. Your letter could languish in the post office while penalties and fees accrue. In our case, the president ignored a certified letter for over two weeks. She finally sent a maintenance worker to the post office to collect it. Hand deliver a copy of your letter to the president and property manager. Obtain complete names (in legible block letters), signatures and the date as confirmation of receipt. If there is an official association stamp, politely request that it be applied to your letter. If your letter is longer than one page, request that each page be initialed.

Bring a Witness. Conduct discussions with Board members about your case in front of at least one <u>neutral</u> witness, preferably a respected fellow owner. Observer(s) should remain quiet during the interaction and provide a signed/dated report soon thereafter. Alternatively, include the full name, date and signature on your <u>record of discussion</u>.

Defend Your Condo & Homeowner Rights!

"Our board members and property manager just don't have a clue. The bottom here line is something that my son told me years ago, 'You can't fix stupid.'"

– HOA member explaining why he decided to move.

Chapter Nine
How to Become a
Homeowner Warrior

Convinced that you've been unfairly targeted by the Board and confident that you can prove it? Then transform yourself into a Homeowner Warrior.

Polish your armor, prepare a protective wall of information and prepare your battle strategy.

Garner Neighborly Support. Speak with neighbors you trust behind closed doors in a calm manner. Let them know you received a warning letter and that you're perplexed.

Quietly Investigate. Did other neighbors violate the association documents and/or rules over the same period without enforcement action? Have Board members broken the rule – and can you prove it? Identify homeowners guilty of the same infraction. For example, I quietly compiled a "secret" list of former and current pet owners.

Defend Your Condo & Homeowner Rights!

Be Persistent. You can't give up. I learned that the deceased sister of a former mayor lived in the building for fifteen years with her pet cats. Although several aged residents remembered the woman, they could not recall her name nor the particular mayor. After many months of discussion, a resident finally remembered the mayor's last name, I reached him by phone and he provided a signed statement. I also discovered over twelve months into the case that a former Board member and his wife took care of their daughter's cats during his tenure as president. Fearing public embarrassment, the former president forbid his wife to tell me! Fortunately, she accidentally "spilled the beans" in a chance discussion about other matters. I also learned along the way that a former Board secretary openly kept parakeets for over a decade.

Contact Fellow Violators. During one such visit, I learned that the president visited the pet owner and saw her cat months before initiating action against me. But she did not demand that the cat be removed. This vital piece of evidence would have been missed if I failed to contact each potential violator and speak with them behind closed doors.

Do Not Disclose. Establish a dialogue of trust. Assure such violators that you will not reveal their identity without their permission. When contacting pet owners,

Defend Your Condo & Homeowner Rights!

I immediately promised not to share their names with the Board. Your near-term goal is information gathering. Your long-term goal is to convince violators to sign corroborating statements.

Do Not Pester. A former board officer who kept parakeets during her tenure was rarely well enough to see me. She was nearly ninety. Her cooperation was vital. I patiently waited about ten days before making each call, politely inquiring when she could meet with me. Exercise self-control. You have everything to lose, but your neighbor has little to gain by helping you.

Do Not Empower. Unfriendly neighbors will ask probing questions in order to elicit a response that can be reported to Board members. Your welfare is not their concern. Their sole objective is to enhance their own prestige at your expense. Moreover, friends can quickly become adversaries when money is at issue. Do not provide ammunition that can later be used against you. Be careful whom you empower with information about your efforts.

Do Not Vent. You're frustrated and naturally want to let off steam. This is an easy mistake to make. Do not "megaphone" your case in the lobby or elevators.

Defend Your Condo & Homeowner Rights!

Guard Informal Words. A clever Board commando will record and use your words to attack you at a later date. "It turned out that a nice woman in the office kept notes on every little thing I said," wrote a reader. If you have no witnesses to the conversation, you have no defense. You might not even recall the words for which you stand accused. Several days after receiving a warning letter, I encountered our association president in the lobby. We had a brief, albeit heated, exchange. Over a year later, her version of my words, to which there were no witnesses, appeared in a motion by the association attorney! Even worse consequences can occur if the Board member has witnesses, but you do not.

Phrases you should never employ in discussions with your president or Board members:

* You're a thief, and I hope you rot in jail.
* You are a lying SOB, and I hope you rot in hell.
* You're crazy and should be institutionalized.
* You're a whore/pimp.
* I'm going to report you to the IRS.
* You better watch your back.
* I hope your tires are full of air because ...

Do Not Spit or Hit. During a board election, one senior member spit at another over a grievance dating back many years. Another tried to hit the board treasurer with a steel object but another member caught her arm.

Hone Your Response Letter. Address the issue and nothing more. Homeowners often rant on for pages with incoherent arguments that undermine their case.

Protect Your Pride. One might refer to it as the "I am naked" syndrome. In a misguided effort to win Board sympathy, a beleaguered owner provided embarrassing details about his wife's mental and physical health. Pathos is not power. Every current and future Board member will have access to your letter, which remains accessible in the association file cabinet virtually forever.

Hold Crucial Cards. Provide as much information as possible without revealing ALL of your supporting documentation. Undisclosed evidence could prove a vital line of defense if your association proceeds with legal action against you.

Certify Your Mail. Your letter must be sent to the association office in a timely basis by certified mail. As discussed above, your letter must be sent prior to the date specified in the warning letter.

Send Copies. Send copies only to Members of the Board and to the property manager. Do not copy your police chief, mayor, local legislators or governor.

Defend Your Condo & Homeowner Rights!

Obtain Confirming Signatures. As noted above, xerox your certified receipt onto a copy of your letter. Ask the association president and property manager to provide their full names, signatures and the date on the letter.

Bring Your Own Witness. Ensure that at least one witness is present when you ask the president and property manager to sign. Do not bring your boyfriend/girlfriend or husband/wife. Ask a respected and preferably neutral neighbor to accompany you. This party should remain quiet at all times and not attempt to argue your case.

Do Not Lose Your Temper. Do not call the president or other Board members a bunch of liars, pigs or thieves when you ask for their signature! The sole purpose of this meeting is to obtain confirmation signatures on your response to the association's letter.

Do Not Email. Do not reply to the warning letter by email under any circumstances.

Do Not Reply to Emails. Email text can be modified and used against you. However, if email exchanges should occur, protect yourself: 1) Save emails in a designated email folder – do not delete them; 2) Print and keep copies in a special file; 3) Use the reply option when you respond in order to maintain the discussion

Defend Your Condo & Homeowner Rights!

thread; 4) Use the <u>least number of words</u> and 5) Do not share your emails with neighbors or send them copies.

Research Your Defense. I spent months researching condo laws and prior arbitration cases in my state. Possible defenses include odd sounding names like Estopple, Laches (no, it's not a cup of coffee), Selective Enforcement, Waiver and Grandfathering. The state bureau regulating condominiums and HOAs should offer a free online database of prior cases. Several legal databases are accessible online for a fee.

However, just because you found a case that "sounds like" yours does not mean that you interpreted the case, defense or the application of the law correctly. And it may have been overruled by a later case. After researching case histories, it's best to consult with an attorney. Organize the material according to each <u>relevant</u> defense. Provide a brief case summary and the entire online citation, if available. A condo or HOA attorney should be familiar with key precedents. However, by doing your own research, you level the playing field and can possibly save money in the future.

Prepare Your Offense. There is also a "knock-out" step you can take. <u>Threaten</u> to sue the Board. As noted above, suing the Board is a complex and costly matter. However, a letter which cooly describes possible Board

75

Defend Your Condo & Homeowner Rights!

violations could derail your opponents. This letter
should be drafted by or prepared on the advice of an
attorney knowledgeable about the laws regulating
condo or homeowner associations in your state.

Chapter Ten
How to Navigate the Legal Maze

Homeowners frequently become hysterical and/or enraged upon receiving a warning letter from the association attorney. It feels like a firecracker exploding in one's brain. Few understand how to respond or whether to hire an attorney to assist in their case. Many ignore the letter. Others reply with verbose content, entreaties and threats.

As discussed earlier, the homeowner is typically given a thirty-day window to comply with the Board's initial warning letter. If the owner does not comply in that time frame and notify the Board of such compliance, a legal warning letter will follow. You are then typically granted an additional fourteen days to comply with the legal warning letter.

It is essential that you or your attorney acknowledge receipt of the legal letter within the time specified. If the violation is something you wish to clear up quickly, then respond immediately and always by certified mail, with return receipt requested. The one thing you should not do is wait until the last moment to seek legal advice.

Defend Your Condo & Homeowner Rights!

And beware! The association is billing you for the attorney's time in issuing that letter. Therefore, you can find yourself in a bizarre situation.

> 1) You comply with the Board's request but fail to notify the Board and therefore receive a legal warning letter from the association attorney.

> 2) You reply to and comply with the legal letter but are then billed by your Board for the attorney's time and costs in writing the legal warning letter.

> 3) You conclude that this legal bill is ridiculous, in light of the fact that you complied, and choose to ignore the bill for the attorney's services.

> 4) The association attorney's fee remains "on the books" and garners interest. You then receive a second legal letter demanding the original fee, interest and a charge for this new letter. What began as a token fee starts multiplying rapidly.

Although you complied with the original request, your failure to pay the attorney's fee means the association can, and likely will, take further legal action against you. An initial legal fee of a few hundred dollars can

78

even result in a lien against your property.

Finding a qualified and affordable attorney is a challenge. Attorneys who represent associations rarely accept individual homeowners as clients. Calls to lawyers throughout the state went unanswered. I even contacted the office of the state legislator representing my district – also an attorney – but he did not return my calls.

Desperate, I phoned condo lawyers around the country. Days were wasted in this fruitless venture. A New York attorney returned my call but declared that she had no working knowledge of Florida condo statutes. After great effort, we identified a handful of qualified Florida attorneys willing to help owners. The first wanted $15,000 to review our file. My file consisted of documents drafted by my Qualified Respondent, a fellow attorney. We learned, however, that attorneys specializing in condominium law are generally wary of files prepared by colleagues from other arenas. The other lawyers quoted similar fees. Astounded, we pressed forward on our own.

To spare readers endless hours in a legal maze, I canvassed a number of lawyers on the dual challenges of responding to the association attorney's warning letter and hiring an attorney to assist in your case. Their

Defend Your Condo & Homeowner Rights!

responses are compiled below. Special appreciation to Florida attorneys Jean Winters and Barry Boca for their contributions to this section.

Q: How much information should the owner provide when responding to the attorney's first warning letter? Should the response be briefly or should it contain key arguments against the charge?

A: There are several issues to consider, but the general rule is the less said the better.

> Case 1: If one has done what is alleged, whether deliberately, accidentally or unintentionally, and you have no intention of repeating it, then apologize briefly – but do not explain why you did it – and promise not to do so again.

> Case 2: If you are guilty of the infraction – if you did what is alleged – and your Board has a history of being litigious, legally aggressive or vicious, then retain an attorney who specializes in these matters.

> Case 3: If you didn't do what is alleged, then simply say that the allegation is incorrect. Do not say more. Do not argue or try to explain why the allegation is wrong. It's up to the

Board's attorney to gather the facts to support his/her allegation. Don't make that task easier.

Q: Are there special circumstances where it is better not to respond to the attorney?

A: No! If you receive a warning letter from an attorney, it generally means that your Board is ready to take action against you.

Q: What type of legal action can my association take?

A: Procedures vary by state. Florida condo associations are required to submit disputes to arbitration prior to taking an owner to court, while homeowner associations must go to mandatory mediation. However, in several instances, the association can take the owner directly to court. Assessments and evictions are two such exceptions. In Florida, if a lien dates back to the original date of the association's covenants, the association can take the owner to court to foreclose the lien. They can also place a lien without going to court, pursuant to both the association's declaration and to Florida statutes.

Q: Can an owner hope to stop the association action in its tracks through legal action?

Defend Your Condo & Homeowner Rights!

A: Yes. A cease and desist injunction is one possibility. Another is a suit against the Board for discrimination. Consider suing the attorney and/or the Board on any number of grounds, such as harassment, and publicizing that action to the community.

Q: Should the owner admit to the infraction if he/she knowingly violated the rule but feels there are mitigating circumstances?

A: There are no mitigating circumstances when dealing with a hungry lawyer or a litigious Board. If you think there are mitigating circumstances, hire an attorney.

Q: Is it absolutely necessary to seek legal counsel before responding to the legal warning letter?

A: You should have an attorney at least review or draft the response for your signature. A letter sent under your attorney's signature might antagonize the Board and make settlement less likely – or it could bring the action to a full stop. It depends on the charge against you.

Q: If the owner responds to the attorney's warning letter without consulting a lawyer, how long should it be?

Defend Your Condo & Homeowner Rights!

A: Your response should be as short as possible, unless written by your attorney. Every word you employ can and will be used against you.

Q: What if the owner is an attorney?

A: Even an owner who is a practicing attorney might want to consult with a lawyer with expertise in association issues. In one recent contentious case, both the husband and wife were practicing attorneys. Worried that they were too emotionally involved, they sought outside legal counsel but did most of the costly legal research by themselves.

Q: The majority of owners believe that they cannot afford to pay legal fees for a response letter, let alone for an entire case. What range of costs are they looking at?

A: Legal fees vary in response to several factors. One should discuss this with the attorney at the outset. Lawyers sell their expertise as a function of the time they devote to a case. Billing rates currently run about $250/hour – though it could be more for senior attorneys and less for junior attorneys. Hourly rates are not the only consideration. A senior attorney might solve the problem much quicker. Law firms also quote higher fees when they don't want to handle a particular issue, case or client.

Defend Your Condo & Homeowner Rights!

Q: How much time should it take to prepare a response?

A: Responding to the legal warning letter could be a simple matter involving a one-hour attorney-client meeting and another hour of the attorney's time to prepare the response letter. However, some situations require more extensive research. What seems simple to a prospective client may be a complex legal situation.

Q: Should the owner meet with the attorney in his/her office or can the discussion be conducted by phone?

A: Most attorneys prefer face-to-face meetings. So should potential clients.

Q: How much might it cost to hire an attorney to handle the entire case?

A: Attorney's fees and expenses for handling a complex case and/or a prolonged case generally range between $30,000 and $150,000. Additionally, if the homeowner loses the case, she/he could face penalties, fines and the possibility of reimbursing the other side for their legal fees and expenses. Proceeding without an attorney, however, could ultimately cost much more.

Defend Your Condo & Homeowner Rights!

Q: What are the chances of winning the case if the homeowner retains the services of a qualified attorney?

A: Relatively few enforcement victims win their case, with or without the services of an attorney.

Q: Are there any other advantages to hiring an attorney?

A: Where money is no object, some distraught homeowners find solace in consulting with an attorney at length, much as they would a psychiatrist.

"You have to have a dream so you can get
up in the morning."

– Billy Wilder

Chapter Eleven
How to Build Your Moat

You've replied to the Board's warning letter(s) and to the association attorney. You began collecting facts about the history of such violations in your building or community.

Now start building your moat with vital case files. Create at least four folders.

Supporting Documentation. The first folder contains every objective piece of supporting documentation – including receipts, records, dates and other pertinent information. I obtained records from our local vet confirming a decade of service at the same address.

Board Communications. The second folder contains warning letters received from the Board and the association attorney, as well as notes on all relevant discussions with Board members.

Board Meeting Jewels. The third folder contains records of Board meetings. Board meetings can be recorded by a non-Board member, so long as it is done publicly, don't hide your recorder. I recorded and personally transcribed half-a-dozen Board meetings.

Yes, it was tedious, but you cannot imagine how helpful it was to have an exact record of what was said. Our president repeatedly stated at Board meetings that she "was not aware of any other pets in the building" when she took enforcement action against our family. Board minutes rarely reflect such. But I had her fly-by-the-lip jewels on tape!

Shortly thereafter, the pet owner mentioned above signed a statement indicating that both the president and another Board member visited her unit months prior to taking action against us, saw her pet cat at the time and did not ask her to remove it.

Others provided similarly damaging statements concerning what the president knew and when she knew it – as opposed to what she said. *"Why does everyone accuse me of lying all of the time?"* was another gem recorded for posterity at a board meeting.

Requests for Association Records. The fourth folder includes requests for association records. Section 718.111(12)(b) Florida Statutes (2002), provides that:

Defend Your Condo & Homeowner Rights!

"The official records of the association shall be maintained within the state. The records of the association shall be made available to a unit owner within 5 working days after receipt of written request by the board or its designee. This paragraph may be complied with by having a copy of the official records of the association available for inspection or copying on the condominium property or association property."

We made numerous requests for documents. The president offered excuses for delays beyond the five-day window. Extending this time period is only allowable in Florida if agreed to by the parties, which was not the case. A Florida association also has the right to charge for the direct cost of copying documents.

Most important, when you arrive for the document viewing, make sure to bring a copy of your original letter of request. Check off each document that you asked for before you leave the room. If you're presented with a large set of files, you will not be able to prove that files were missing unless you checked them off at the time and the president initialed the missing file. Bring a tape recorder. Ask the Board president to confirm that the file is missing on tape and demand that he/she initial the missing file on your original letter.

Defend Your Condo & Homeowner Rights!

Section 718.111(12)(c), Florida Statutes also states that a unit owner who is denied access to official records is entitled to the actual damages or minimum damages for the association's willful failure to comply with this paragraph. "The minimum damages shall be $50 per calendar day up to 10 days, the calculation to begin on the 11th working day after receipt of the written request."

The actual fine, in our case, was written in invisible ink. We repeatedly filed motions regarding the failure to provide documents, which the Arbitrator simply chose to ignore.

Corroborating Statements. The fifth folder could be the most crucial in building your case. It contains original supporting or corroborating statements by your neighbors. A maintenance worker, who should have feared for his job, signed a statement indicating that pets had been in the building throughout his seventeen years of service and that our cat had resided in the building longer than many owners. For added security, a set of copies of all statements should be kept outside of your home or in a lock box at your bank. I gave a complete set to a trusted neighbor.

Statements are not easy to prepare. This is what you must do:

Defend Your Condo & Homeowner Rights!

Prepare Drafts. Don't ask your neighbor to draft his or her statement. It will never happen. After speaking with your neighbor, draft the statement yourself and present it to the party for his/her signature. An attorney can help devise the most effective language. But don't waste precious money on attorney meetings and calls until you briefly detail what neighbors are likely to sign. Note the word "briefly." Statements should be no more than one or two pages.

Convince Supporters to Sign. Convincing neighbors to sign a statement is an excruciating process. What should take a few minutes can turn into bottomless hours filled with stories about their former lives, their children and every possible honor bestowed upon their grandchildren. You will be sitting at the edge of the couch, temples pounding – as if your entire world depended on this moment. If you depart their home without a signature, there may not be a second chance. Given more time, neighbors are less likely, not more likely, to assist. Remember, you need their full name, date and signature.

Defend Your Condo & Homeowner Rights!

Ensure Witness Signatures. Statements should also be notarized. This is extremely difficult to achieve unless you have a friend or colleague who is a notary and is also willing to accompany you on door-to-door visits to collect statements. Your fellow owners are likely to be intimidated by the prospect of traveling to a bank or other institution where a notary can be found. At the very least, have a witness on hand for the signing of each statement – other than yourself. Place three lines on the statement for your witness: full name, date and signature.

Notarize, Notarize. We did not attempt to notarize our statements for the reasons outlined above – using witnesses instead. Moreover, I personally phoned the DBPR in August 2005 (kept notes on the call) to ask whether the statements should be notarized. The answer was no! Yet, in the final hour – fourteen months after submitting our first set of statements and with only a matter of days remaining until the Final Hearing – the association attorney petitioned for a dismissal for all our statements as hearsay – because they were not notarized and thus not legitimate affidavits.

Although the Arbitrator rejected the attorney's position, he stated for the very first time that while his department did not <u>require</u> notarization, non-notarized statements <u>were only valid if the person providing the</u>

<u>statement testified at the Final Hearing!</u> We were stunned by the veil surrounding such a key issue – one vital to our defense. As there was zero chance we could convince elderly witnesses to notarize their statements in the short time remaining, we faced dire straits if they failed to appear at the hearing! Another lesson learned about Arbitration 101.

An association attorney, by contrast, has a strong advantage in obtaining notarized statements. He can request that Board members visit his office on a single occasion – or he can bring a notary to a closed-door meeting of the Board.

Our property manager was also a notary, making it very easy for the association attorney to ensure that all Board statements were notarized. On the other hand, Florida law provides that "you may not be the notary for a transaction in which you have a financial interest or to which you are a party." Since the property manager was a key figure in our case – the party who first advised the president to take action against us – one wonders at the use of his services in this instance.

Be Alert for Suspicious Affidavits. You will be held to the highest standard in preparing and obtaining signatures on affidavits. Board members, by contrast, might follow a different set of rules: namely, their own.

Defend Your Condo & Homeowner Rights!

Several of our Board members brazenly misrepresented facts on their statements, because they feared little consequence – that is, until we made it abundantly clear that perjury on a notarized statement is a punishable offense. Their fear of perjury charges may have contributed to our victory.

When asked why she signed the affidavit against us, our Board treasurer repeatedly argued, "I sign what our president tells me to sign." She later resorted to a second excuse, as captured in this memorable exchange:

Treasurer: "I signed the affidavit without reading it, because I didn't have my glasses on at the time."

President: "You didn't have to read it (the affidavit). I read it to you."

A new Board president was elected in January 2006. Exasperated by the "glasses" rationale, he told the treasurer: "You have four pairs of glasses here – three on the table, and you're wearing one of them. Yet, you repeatedly claimed that you didn't know what you signed in the Starr case because you didn't have your glasses. You cannot use your missing glasses as a continuing excuse to say that you don't know what you're signing."

Defend Your Condo & Homeowner Rights!

The treasurer responded: "You're so mean."

To which the president replied: "No, I'm not mean. I'm conducting myself as the president of this Board."

Don't get excited, dear reader. Within a few weeks, the new president (who was actually a previously dethroned president) accused the new property manager of insulting him and demanded that the management firm immediately replace the property manager. Owners were up in arms once again. They felt the new manager was doing an excellent job. Moreover, our documents did not allow the president to fire an employee without a board vote.

Only three weeks of taking office, the new president threw the building into complete chaos and violated our documents. The good news: old enemies soon joined forces to stop this abuse of power.

Herein lies an important lesson.

Board oppressors join forces with their victims given the right conditions. Take your fight to a higher level by sticking to the issue rather than personalizing the situation. Above all, don't use derogatory or belittling names. Defamation of character won't help, but the Board member might help you down the line. Civility reigns supreme. The following case graphically demonstrates how the situation can rocket out of control. (Santa Monica Condo. Assoc., Inc. v. O'Connor, Final Order/ July 31, 2002):

> "The association proved that one of the unit owners and his guests have created a nuisance by engaging in behavior that resulted in an attempt by the respondents' guest to enter another owner's unit, an infestation of ants in the downstairs neighbors' unit, a verbal attack on a realtor, the dumping of urine on one of the downstairs neighbors, the soiling of another owner's parking spot and numerous other incidents."

Nuisance claims and suits can flow two ways. Dust from a condo renovation infiltrated a neighbor's unit. Claiming that it cost $52,000 in cleaning bills to remove the dust, he forwarded the bills to the condo owner and sued to recover the money. The disgruntled neighbor lost the case and soon thereafter sold his apartment to the "offender."

Chapter Twelve
Mandatory Arbitration 101

My brother lives and works in London. He's a senior partner in a demanding legal practice. With a five-hour time difference between us, we often communicated at midnight his time or thereafter.

While a member in good standing of the New York, Washington and Chicago Bars – and accredited to appear before the Supreme Court – he is not a member of the Florida Bar. The DBPR therefore required that he represent our case as a "Qualified Representative." He filled out the requisite form, and we took our first step into the quicksand of mandatory arbitration.

A Florida court of appeals noted: "The laudatory goals of the [Federal Arbitration Act] will be achieved only to the extent that courts ensure arbitration is an alternative to litigation, not an additional layer in a protracted contest." By contrast, many refer to mandatory condo arbitration and HOA mediation as leaving the country without a passport. The homeowner is assumed guilty unless he/she has the guts, money and perseverance to prove otherwise.

Defend Your Condo & Homeowner Rights!

The emotional and physical drain of our multi-year arbitration battle cannot be overstated. Before the association finally gave up, we made thirty-five filings of over nine hundred pages.

My case required voluminous research, complex motions and counter-motions in multiple drafts, over two thousand emails, lengthy investigations and the preparation of dozens of witness statements supporting our defense. We also: filed numerous requests for association documents; coordinated two arbitration hearings, scheduling over thirty witnesses on each occasion and confronted obstructive tactics by the attorney and by Board members that would have exhausted any but the most resolute adversary.

Our initial February 10, 2005 "Answer to the Original Petition," enumerated many of our defenses, cited numerous legal precedents and included twenty-two exhibits – key witness statements – that supported our case. However, both the association attorney and the Arbitrator ignored our initial defenses and exhibits.

The Board's attorney apparently made little effort to determine the facts or the legitimacy of the association's case before proceeding. Instead, he made repeated filings containing erroneous or seriously misleading statements. By his own admission, the Arbitrator did not read our supporting evidence in depth until the final phase of the case.

At the beginning of this ordeal, we knew nothing about the mandatory arbitration process. By the end, we had thousands of hours of unwanted experience.

Here are the highlights:

Plaintiff vs Respondent. The party who initiates an arbitration or mediation case is the Plaintiff. The defending side is called the Respondent. If your association files an arbitration or mediation action against, you're the Respondent. If you file against the association, you're the Plaintiff. In several instances, associations have filed actions against Board members in their personal capacities.

The Arbitrator: In Florida, Department of Business and Professional Regulation Arbitrators have more power than judges, because the judiciary is at least accountable to the public and to the press. As of the publication of this book, the credentials and backgrounds of DBPR Arbitrators are unavailable on the DBPR website. I also conducted advanced internet searches under the name of our Arbitrator, to no avail. An attorney by the same name once worked for a small Florida county. Otherwise, the man had no public record to call upon.

Where did he earn his law degree? What was his relationship to the association attorney handling our case? Did they go to school together?

Protracted Process. The DBPR claims that most decisions are rendered on a timely basis. However, if you become impoverished or your health is destroyed in a protracted process – the Arbitrator takes months or, as in our case, more than a year to make a decision – it's of absolutely no consequence to the Arbitrator or the DBPR.

Complicated Communications: We were informed that all communications between my Qualified Representative and the Arbitrator must be sent by fax, on the rationale that email communications are not reliable. He could send text and attachments by email but was required to fax a hard copy of every single page! Moreover, he was also required to send copies of every motion, counter-motion and all other communications to the association attorney by fax. Sending over 100 pages plus appendices on numerous occasions, his fax machine often burned well into the night! Dealing with multiple attachments, someone had to handle and watch over the transmissions to assure that they went through in an orderly manner.

<u>Here was the rub</u>. The DBPR is not authorized to fax or phone outside of the United States. All responses from the DBPR were sent overseas by snail mail – leading to frequent delays caused by bad weather or insufficient postage. The association attorney, by contrast, received instant copies of all DBPR communications by fax.

Filing Dates: The Respondent is required to file no later than the date specified by the Arbitrator, or provide an airtight reason for being unable to do so. Association attorneys, by contrast, are held to a different standard. The association attorney missed several filing dates and sent copies of his motions to my representative at the wrong office address, apparently without fear of sanction. My Qualified Representative wrote:

"Whether willful, intentional or a result of neglect, this repeated and flagrant breach of the DBRP's Rules, should be sanctioned by the Arbitrator, and if appropriate at this stage of the case, by entry of a default as provided in Rule 61B-45.020."

Bedfellows. The Arbitrator ignored repeated requests to sanction the attorney for his behavior. There is a logical explanation. Arbitrators are attorneys. Florida Arbitrators and association attorneys are thus bedfellows of the same elite club, sometimes quite literally. One Arbitrator was married to the senior partner in a high-profile law firm that represented numerous community associations. For a non-Florida based attorney to prevail against this inner sanctum was a rare feat indeed.

Accountability. The typical homeowner fights a scorching battle without boots or battle gear. However, if an Arbitrator's decision against the homeowner is later overturned by the courts, there is no black mark on his record. The Arbitrator is simply a government employee doing his job.

The Case Management Conference. An Arbitration Case Management Conference is a typically a teleconference between the Arbitrator, the association attorney and the Respondent's attorney, or in our case, the Qualified Representative for the Respondent. We were told that Plaintiffs and Respondents were **not permitted to participate** in Case Management Conference calls if represented by legal counsel.

However, through a Board member's chance remark, we learned that the association attorney invited Board members to listen in on every call! We had failed to ask the Arbitrator the right question: Can the respondent **listen in on the call?** The Arbitrator saw no compelling reason to reveal this insider knowledge, unless specifically asked.

The homeowner who chooses to represent himself/herself must participate in the call and will be up against two attorneys – the association attorney and the Arbitrator! Words should be carefully measured.

Record the Call. Why? The Arbitrator did not record or provide transcripts of these Case Management Conference calls. He kept notes – which he did not share – and issued rulings based on those notes. **There was no official record of what was said.** We understood that summaries would be provided, but none were offered. The Arbitrator explained that it is perfectly legitimate for the Plaintiff or Respondent to record calls, but he wasn't going to do so.

In one of our Case Management Conference calls, the Arbitrator declared that the association attorney would not be allowed to take certain actions. Yet, in a subsequent Official Order, the Arbitrator reversed his position. We did not tape the conversation. Therefore, we had no proof that the Arbitrator contradicted himself.

Defend Your Condo & Homeowner Rights!

Good Night's Rest. One or two teleconferences were scheduled in the afternoon hour for the convenience of the Arbitrator, although it was dinner time or later for my representative. An early morning teleconference in Florida often resulted in planning discussions at 1:00 a.m or 2:00 a.m London time. My Qualified Representative wrote: "I suggest we speak around 7-8 a.m. your time Tuesday to prepare for the 9 a.m teleconference with the Arbitrator. If you don't hear from me by 8:15 a.m, please call me, as I might have fallen asleep at my desk!"

Chapter Thirteen
Final Hearing: Can You Hear?

The Arbitrator normally makes his final decision on an enforcement case after holding a Final Hearing. The hearing is attended by: the plaintiff, which in our case was the association; the respondent; attorneys for both sides; expert witnesses, if any, and other witnesses. The hearing takes place on the association premises or at the attorney's office, if acceptable to both parties. It can also be held at the Arbitrator's office if reasonably close by.

Our Arbitrator, however, was based in Tallahassee, a plane ride away. We were initially informed that he would preside over the hearing by phone and would remain on the line irrespective of how many hours the call might take. We received the following order:

> "The Arbitrator hereby requests that the parties submit three alternative dates in February 2005, during which they will be available for a Final Hearing in the above referenced matter. The Arbitrator intends to conduct the Final Hearing by telephone. If [the Qualified Representative] so wishes, he may also appear via telephone, provided that he initiates contact with the final

hearing site. The parties shall submit their proposed dates by 5:00 p.m. on January 13, 2005, failing which the Arbitrator will choose a date."

There was only one speaker phone in the association meeting room. It used the association's fax line. How could the Arbitrator conduct an eight-hour hearing on this single phone? How would our out-of-town witness – allowed to address the hearing by cell phone – speak to the Arbitrator when he was on another line?

Urgent client matters initially made it difficult for my Qualified Representative to depart the UK and arrive in Florida for the early morning hearing. We feared he would be compelled to interview witnesses from London by phone! He wrote to me:

"How will it work if the Arbitrator is on a phone link up and I am too? Separate lines? Same line? How do I conduct an eight-hour phone hearing, and can it be technically arranged? If the Arbitrator appears by phone, can his office can arrange a conference link to a number that I can phone? Or do I have to initiate the phone call to both the Arbitrator and the meeting room and pay conference call rates from the UK?"

Defend Your Condo & Homeowner Rights!

Frazzled hours and a barrage of emails later, the Arbitrator agreed to fly from Tallahassee to Miami for the <u>first</u> Final Hearing. (He also consented to do so months later for the reconvened Final Hearing.) My representative juggled his busy legal practice so that he could conduct the hearing in Florida.

To our chagrin, we were informed that the burden fell on us (in other words, on the victim) – and not on the Plaintiff (the association) to organize the hearing! It was a grueling process. These are the steps you must follow:

* **Hire a Subpoena Server.** In order to compel supporters and opponents to appear at a condo arbitration Final Hearing, the homeowner must hire a reliable subpoena server willing to deliver subpoenas directly to all recipients and not leave them under doors.

* **Hire a Court Reporter.** If you later appeal an Arbitrator's final ruling and proceed to court, personal recordings and/or transcripts of the final hearing will be inadmissible. You must pay for the court reporter's time and for the final transcript produced.

Defend Your Condo & Homeowner Rights!

* The Hearing. Plan for a hearing that lasts an hour or continues over several days. The length of the hearing is entirely up to the Arbitrator. Moreover, you cannot present new evidence at the hearing, even if you think it's vital to your case. If the information was not presented as part of your initial defense(s) and filings, the Arbitrator will not allow you or your attorney to raise it at the hearing. Further, if you raised several possible defenses, but the Arbitrator ruled against one or more during the course of your case, you cannot present evidence on these matters at the hearing.

* Coordinate Schedules. I've organized numerous international conferences, but never encountered such unusual and personalized scheduling demands. One star witness, for example, would not appear on a Friday; it conflicted with her favorite day at the race track. Another could only appear at 9:00 a.m., lest the hearing interfere with a regular golf date. One witness was tied up until noon daily playing tennis. Several witnesses had back-to-back medical appointments on certain days and wanted to leave other days open "just in case" they had to see a doctor. Almost every witness had a "preferable" hour.

* **Prepare Multiple Copies of Witness Statements.** You must provide a complete set of witness statements for the Arbitrator and for the court reporter. Each witness must be given an advance copy of his/her statement. If the witness cannot read the statement into the record, you or your attorney can do it on their behalf – but only if the witness is present at the hearing!

* **Plan the Arbitrator's Lunch.** We were told to plan for an hour lunch break each day of the hearing. Should we have food available or risk the possibility that the association attorney would take the Arbitrator out for lunch? If we purchased food in advance, would this be viewed as a bribe? Were we required to supply food for the association attorney and his colleagues? We knew he would have at least one co-counsel present. We contacted the DBPR secretary to determine whether the Arbitrator wanted us to provide lunch and what kind of food he preferred to eat!

All of the above tasks were completed in a timely manner and the schedule was firmly in place. The association attorney then employed another delaying tactic.

Defend Your Condo & Homeowner Rights!

Less than forty-eight hours before the Final Hearing – with my representative literally on his way to the airport – he convinced the Arbitrator to delay the hearing by several additional months. All that work for nothing. We would have to suffer through the agony once again!

Why did the Arbitrator agree to the delay? The attorney claimed that the postponement would allow association members to vote on removing the no-pet clause from our original documents. A favorable vote would resolve the issue and end the need for a hearing. We argued that this was just another sordid delaying tactic that would cost time and money. It was further indication that the Board and its counsel feared or knew they would lose at the hearing. Again, the Arbitrator ruled in the association's favor, and this charade continued.

The proposed amendment called for allowing "a cat in every unit" – ridiculous language that was unlikely to hold up in court of law even if approved. The Board organized the vote. However, ballots were returned directly to the attorney's office. Predictably, at a meeting called to announce the outcome – a Board meeting that was not officially a Board meeting – the attorney stated that there were insufficient votes to open the envelopes. And so he concluded, the vote had failed. Seventy-five percent or at least 108 of the 144 unit owners were required to vote. Only 94 actually voted, 14 less than the required 108.

We soon discovered that many unit owners did not receive a ballot. At that point, we argued that this "error" was grounds for dismissal of the case. We also stressed that association members were not invited to help solicit votes and, in fact, were discouraged from doing so. Moreover, some of the envelopes were sent overseas (to Israel, Europe and Canada). There was no way that they could have arrived and been returned in the brief time frame allowed.

The Board decided that it was not worth their time to make the effort to reach another fifty voters. The ballot vote didn't fail; the Board failed the ballot. The Arbitrator remain unmoved by our arguments for dismissal and rescheduled the "final" Final Hearing for the following month. Numerous owners demanded that the ballots be transferred back to the association, but the attorney failed to do so.

"Little things affect little minds."

– Benjamin Disraeli

Chapter Fourteen
How to Master the Subpoena Mystery

How does the homeowner prepare and issue subpoenas for condo arbitration? The arbitration subpoena was a deep mystery. But we had to solve it. No fact sheet was available at the time of our case, and there may not be one when you read this book. When I first inquired with the DBPR, I was told that we had to follow "court procedures," but given no further roadmap.

Subpoenas are normally issued through the court system. After repeated calls to the District Court, a deputy clerk finally gave me a lucid answer. She stated:

"If you do not have pending civil matter in the court, our office cannot issue your subpoenas. For the clerks' office to issue the subpoena, you must open a civil action – which means you must file a law suit. The DBPR did not give you the full picture. While you do have a right to issue a subpoena, they may have failed to explain that you cannot do so through our office unless you open a civil case. We cannot issue your summons, and neither the sheriff's office nor a process server will issue a summons without a case number in the court system."

Many telephone calls later, I learned that our Arbitrator had the authority to issue subpoenas. **Once again, his office failed to provide this vital piece of information until I posed the question in precisely the right way.** The bottom line: I had to research the answer to death before I could arrive at the question. This is what I found.

Defendants Foot the Bill. Moreover, I learned that we were required to foot the bill for the subpoenas! This expense would not be reimbursed unless we <u>prevailed</u> in the case. We incurred over $750 in costs for delivery of subpoenas, which was reimbursed when we were declared the prevailing party.

Defendants Prepare the Text. We provided the text and address for each subpoena, sending the Arbitrator our final copies by zip file. He then signed his name and sent them out. Need I recount the time we wasted in this tedious task?

Defend Your Condo & Homeowner Rights!

Subpoena Hostile Witnesses. We issued subpoenas to hostile witnesses (Board Directors), to assure that they would answer our questions at the hearing.

Reissuing Subpoenas. When the Final Hearing was rescheduled, we were at a loss over how to proceed. Could the prior subpoenas be employed and, if so, how? Could we simply we strike out the date? Who would deliver them the second time around? We initially paid a professional subpoena process server to hand deliver each subpoena. It cost over $750. Would we be forced to pay once again? Hours were spent chasing down the answer from the Arbitrator by email. We also had to fax a copy of each email to both the Arbitrator and the association attorney for their records. My representative wrote to the Arbitrator:

> "The Final Hearing has now been rescheduled for March 2, 2006. Respondent Joyce Starr has contacted your office to understand the procedure for service of subpoenas in these circumstances. She was advised by your office that in the case of each of the subpoenas previously authorized by the Arbitrator and previously served, it will be sufficient merely to strike out the originally scheduled date and time and insert the new date and time.

"I also understand that copies of these subpoenas may be delivered/sent under cover of a letter from the undersigned, as Authorized Representative of Respondents, noting that the date of the Final Hearing has been rescheduled, and requesting the appearance of the person previously served. As regards subpoenas previously authorized by the Arbitrator but not yet served, Respondent Joyce Starr understands the advice from your office to be that it will be sufficient to strike out the originally scheduled date and time and insert the new date and time, and to serve these subpoenas in the usual manner.

"If the foregoing is correct, can you please so confirm by reply email, for good order's sake, as this situation does not appear to be addressed in Ch 61B-45 F.A.C. or any published DBPR Rules. If the foregoing is not correct, can your office please advise the correct procedure to be followed as regards subpoenas in this situation."

Storing Motions and Counter-Motions. My representative purchased a suitcase on wheels to lug our arbitration papers back and forth to his office. This suitcase contained over thirty-five motions and counter-motions. It also held rulings by the arbitrator and responses by the association attorney. With little time or patience to search through the suitcase, he often demanded that I come up with a particular document at the last possible hour.

There was little room in my crowded condo to organize and store my set of documents. My solution was to purchase large Haitian straw baskets. Then I filed each motion or issue by date and separated one from another by colorful pieces of printing paper. The Haitian baskets and color coding added an interesting touch of decor to my home. My cat, by contrast, viewed the paper contents as alternative kitty litter; once again that his instincts were on target.

Undertaking Legal Research. My representative informed me, "I have no time for the research. You will have to give me what I asked for, namely the constituent factual elements/points that need to be proved/adduced for each of the affirmative defenses, such as Selective Enforcement, Waiver, Estoppel, Laches. I want detailed information on what we need to prove and how to win on each of the defenses. Get into the cases themselves. Don't rely only on the summaries." In other words, my professional life as an author, publisher and consultant was now on hold. I was forced to transform myself into a full-time paralegal, without pay and on-call 24/7 for the subsequent year.

The typical homeowner engaged in an Board dispute will encounter a similar challenge. If one attempts to pursue an enforcement case without legal assistance, legal research will likely become a full time job (or obsession). If you invest in attorney, he must still be supremely knowledgeable about all possible defenses – if for no other reason than to save you the expense on research. It took months just to investigate and examine the wide range of possible defenses and related cases, to compare our situation to these cases and to decide upon the best course of action. In attorney-speak, our case would easily have cost over $150,000 in direct legal and paralegal fees – and twice that amount if we lost!

Fortunately, our cat had the services of a savvy attorney, albeit one with no former condo law experience, and an untrained but intensely committed paralegal.

Chapter Fifteen
Right in the Face of Evil

The greatest personal losses in association battles are hope and health. Commandos gleefully shoot poison arrows through your heart and think nothing of it. A relative wrote: "What a way to live one's life. I will be so glad when this is over. It is too much for one's system, and I fear that the two of you will crash. Being right in the face of evil helps energize one, but it is not the whole story. Thank goodness for the Starr genes."

The situation is often so mean-spirited and illogical that it defies understanding. A homeowner wrote to me: "My life is effectively over on every level. Who cares if I live or die or have a stroke or a heart attack or end up in the poor house. I don't see life the way I did before. This case has destroyed my life. I have not had one minute of joy, of friendship. I have never been so attacked and isolated. They destroyed the life I had. I am getting weaker by the day, by the hour. My insides are like shards of glass."

Board tactics and neighborly reactions can put justice to shame. For example, we repeatedly asked the Board and our neighbors questions that fell on deaf ears:

> * Why was this enforcement action taken without prior Board authorization, as numerous statements demonstrated and the Board eventually conceded?

> * Why was this the first pet enforcement action taken by the Board since the building was first occupied in the mid-1970s – and when former Boards had a policy and practice of non-enforcement of the so-called "no-pets" clause of our Condominium Declaration?

> * Why was this absurd and colossal waste of association funds allowed to continue while mold remediation was put on hold?

The Arbitrator even allowed our Board to approve its enforcement action against us retroactively. You read that correctly. How could the Board 'ratify' action taken almost a year prior by two of its members, without formal Board approval – an action based on misrepresentations and falsehoods at the outset?

Was that legally possible? Apart from the legalities, was it morally right?

If the Board failed to properly authorize or approved actions taken at the time, weren't they guilty of basic misrepresentation and of lying? We argued that the true purpose of retroactive ratification action was to protect Board members who wanted to cover their tracks and avoid personal legal liability for wrongful actions.

For the first time in our association's history, the Board hired a policeman to monitor a Board meeting – the so-called Special Meeting to retroactively approve the enforcement action against me a year prior. The association attorney even arranged to videotape the session. Aside from intimidating residents, he might have had a darker objective. The attorney naturally assumed that, as a member of the Board, I would participate in the meeting and vigorously protest the proceedings. Were the police and video tape on-hand to catch me in the act?

Fortunately, since the meeting was convened without proper notice, I did not attend. The Board secretary of also refused to participate for the same reason. Their ploy failed. My representative wrote to the attorney and to the Arbitrator: "Sending in the police? Were the Gang of Five hoping that Joyce Starr would be carried off in handcuffs for "disrupting" the nicely planned "meeting" and have it captured on video?"

Defend Your Condo & Homeowner Rights!

One member supposedly cast her vote by phone, although it was soon discovered that the phone was not connected, and no one was on the line.

But the outcome will come as little surprise. The Arbitrator approved the horrific way the meeting was conducted, along with the Board's action's in retroactively approving the enforcement action. The moral of the story: abusive Boards and their attorneys can even turn back the clock and get away with it.

No less ironic, based on the farcical vote, the association attorney decided not to mount a defense at the Final Hearing. He told the Arbitrator in the next Case Management Conference call: "From the condo's perspective, we have proven that she has a pet and that the declaration says no pets. If we can accept that, we do not need to mount a defense."

His confidence was premature.

Chapter Sixteen
When Board Members Bark

One of the most shocking aspects of this case involved a Board member who was a former president, vice president, and secretary of the Board. Despite being one of the most vociferous proponents of the enforcement action against us, he had harbored his girlfriend's dog in his apartment for over four years and continued to do so. A number of building owners also saw the girlfriend with the dog.

Until this day, I cannot explain what transformed a friendly neighbor harboring a dog into a persecutor trying to destroy a cat. This same Board member also chaired the farcical meeting to retroactively approve the enforcement action against me. Even more outrageous, he brought the canine to the meeting where the Board voted on 'grand-fathering' my cat! I snapped a photo with the dog on his lap. The dog appears to be the one barking, though we can't be sure. The attorney threatened to sue me for capturing this absurdity on film, because I took the picture on association property. Could it get any more bizarre than that?

123

Defend Your Condo & Homeowner Rights!

One of the most egregious Board demands, shockingly conveyed by the attorney and ignored by the Arbitrator, was that I be exiled from the building within thirty days and that no relative of mine ever be allowed to rent or own a unit in the building! Neither the attorney nor the Board had any legal right to make such an outrageous demand.

Moreover, the key signatory to the case, as I accidentally found out, was still furious at my father for two reasons. When she first moved in decades earlier, he allegedly told her that dogs were not permitted. This was technically correct. However, he did not threaten to enforce the rule, and she did not bring her beloved little pet dog into the condo. Secondly, as treasurer and ever mindful of expenses, he insisted that she stop turning on lights in the lobby during daylight hours. Moving into the building from a huge home where she could do as she pleased, the request apparently made her livid. I'm not sure which of his statements she viewed as the greater offense. She never forgave him.

A third Board member was simply afraid of cats. She told me that a "cat jumped at me when I was pregnant, and I never forgot it." Mind you, this was approximately forty years ago. A fifth member was angry over my mold warnings, fearing that our condo values would be reduced if word spread that the building were mold-ridden. Early in the case, he told me that, "You can be sued for saying such things in public." He was also a stickler for detail. If the documents prohibited pets, then there should be no pets, irrespective of failure to enforce over prior decades. He saw it as a black and white issue.

There you have it. Two years of my life and $30,000 in association funds were frittered away because of personal power struggles, old vendettas, primal fears and the bottom line. Approximately $25,000 of that amount was wasted on my case. An additional $5,000 was spent pursuing two other owners to "prove" that the Board was not "selectively enforcing" against me. The DBPR declared the cases moot and dismissed them. The association did not recover a dime.

Both owners were from foreign countries and could barely read English. The first involved retribution against the Russian-born cat owner who provided a statement in our defense. Feeling personally responsible for what transpired, we shouldered her case as well. Since she could not write in English and could not afford an attorney, we drafted her response to the attorney's warning letter and to the letter she received from the Arbitrator. Shortly thereafter, she moved from the building for other reasons. Based on her response to the arbitration letter, the case was declared moot, and she was not required to pay attorney fees.

The second case was so sad that it bears repeating in greater detail. An elderly Hispanic woman lovingly cared for two parakeets owned by her daughter, who died of cancer. Following is an excerpt of the statement provided by the owner (with names removed).

"I do hereby state, declare and confirm:

"1) I have been living here for five years. I kept two parakeets in my unit for over two years. My daughter who passed away [from cancer] left me these parakeets, and they are a great source of comfort. They keep my mind active in facing a deep depression over the loss of my daughter. I keep them on my balcony in full view of anyone who enters the building. No one ever complained.

"2) In late October 2004, Joyce Starr told me that she had received a document stating that she had to remove her cat, which as far as I am aware was kept in her unit and never caused any problems.

"3) This troubled me greatly because I thought that it was acceptable to keep parakeets. I contacted the Board president, hoping that there would be no problems about my pet birds.

"4) I also discussed this matter with my doctor. My psychiatrist gave me a note to hand to the Board president stating that, "Due to mental health issues" I should be allowed to keep my pet birds.

"5) That same week, I presented the president with a copy of this letter. She told me that since I had volunteered this information, she had no choice except to take action against me and that my doctor's note didn't mean a thing. She treated me like dirt. She also met my daughter many years ago when she was undergoing chemotherapy and she lost all of her hair.

"6) The president should have had compassion. But she is a heartless woman. I soon received an unsigned document stating that it came from the Board of Directors of the Condominium, demanding that I remove my pet parakeets, and thereafter a menacing letter from the Condominium's lawyers demanding the same. The parakeets were removed. Until now, they are being kept by my son-in-law.

"7) This entire matter has made me terribly unhappy. I do not know why she behaved in such a cruel manner. My doctor can confirm the terrible emotional distress I suffered as a result of this situation."

The day after we prevailed in our case, the two parakeets were returned to her condo balcony, where they chirp away in peace and harmony.

Board abusers undermine fellow commandos with the same alacrity and imperious attitude. Our former vice-president usurped the power of the woman who was president at the time. In turn, the ex-president, now vice-president, usurped the power of the new Board president by authorizing a new subpoena for our Final Hearing. The dialogue that ensued is illustrative of intra-Board abuse.

New President: "I was elected as president in January. At the time, you told me that the former Board vice president authorized legal expenses behind your back during your presidency. You emphasized that the president is the only person who has the authority to speak with our attorneys. When did you give this authorization for a subpoena to this person?!"

Defend Your Condo & Homeowner Rights!

Vice President (Ex-President): "She wasn't on the witness list, so I decided to call her."

Treasurer to the New President: "She can do what she wants. It's her case."

President to Vice President: "You've usurped my authority."

The vice president pulled out a piece of paper and began writing a letter of resignation.

President: "Are you resigning?"

Vice President: "Yes."

The president briefly departed the room to speak with an owner standing at the door. By the time he returned, the letter of resignation had disappeared.

President: "Where is your letter of resignation?"

Vice President: "She (the treasurer) made me tear it up."

President: Do you want to resign?

Vice President: "Yes."

President: "Then I accept your resignation."

Vice President: "Well, I don't know if I want to resign now."

Shortly after we prevailed in our case, a recall action was launched against the Board. The Board was not recalled because they spent over $30,000 in an effort to silence a whistleblower or because they ignored pressing maintenance problems for over two years.

The recall was sparked by an internal Board dispute over keys. The new Board president, in office for one month, decreed that Board members who were not officers should no longer have keys to the association office and took a number of unilateral actions that angered his Board colleagues. Fellow Board members threw him out of office after one month for "arrogant actions."

His dismissal sparked an intense and well-organized recall action. The recall cost the association yet another $11,000 in legal fees when the Board contested the recall results. Between October 2004 and January 2007, our Board spent over $40,000 on frivolous legal fees but nothing on mold remediation. Ironically, the Board president who pursued the frivolous pet enforcement cases and failed to file over a million dollars in insurance claims was not recalled. Her term later expired.

Association members were unwilling to fight Board abuse of their money, neighbors and building for the prior two years. Earlier efforts to recall Board members had failed. Yet, they eagerly organized and signed this recall petition when an internal Board dispute pitted a younger man against several elderly women over a minor issue.

They attempted to recall a woman who served with distinction for twelve years and ran again at the age of 89, because she wanted to put a stop to the Board's tyranny. One might call it throwing out granny with the bathwater.

"We are on earth to do good for others. What the others are here for I do not know."

– W. H. Auden

Chapter Seventeen
Who is Barking Now?

Fearing exposure and humiliation at the Final Hearing – now only days away – the Board called a Special Meeting on February 27, 2006 to vote on whether or not to grandfather my cat into the building. Over forty homeowners assembled in the meeting room.

Just as the Special Meeting was to begin, the association attorney called an emergency Attorney-Client Privilege session with the Board. Association boards can hold closed door meetings with their attorneys to discuss potential or actual litigation. Although a Member of the Board, I was not allowed into the room because I was the Respondent in the legal action under discussion, namely enforcement of the no-pet rule.

This sudden "emergency" session upset unit owners who had been waiting patiently for the public session to begin. They were especially infuriated that a board member had the gall to bring a dog into the closed meeting – and felt that the attorney poured gasoline on the fire by allowing this to happen.

Defend Your Condo & Homeowner Rights!

The attorney claimed the purpose of the litigation meeting was to discuss the Board's vote on the arbitration case. I was later advised that he spent half the time maligning the Qualified Representative for the Respondent. But this is just hearsay. Clearly, he did not demand that the dog be removed from the association office, because it was still there when residents came pounding on the door forty minutes later.

Elderly citizens were irate. Some began shouting, "We're also your clients" and demanded that they be let into the room. A Board member opened the door a sliver and chaos followed. Residents poured into the tiny office.

The attorney instructed the Board's vice president to call the police for the third time in three months. She complained to the police operator that Board members feared for their safety. The majority of owners present were over seventy years of age. The arrival of the police minutes later put an end to the closed door meeting. The Board moved back into the meeting room and the new president called the session to order. Residents were still furious about the dog. The former vice president acknowledged publically for the first time that the dog was his girlfriend's pet. But he also said the dog belonged to him, that his girlfriend lived with him and that the dog had been living in the parking lot all along! I have it all on tape.

The Board finally took a vote. **It passed four to three. A single vote decided the issue.** My cat, along with other pets currently in residence, was officially grandfathered into the building. The entire episode was so confusing that my single Board supporter – who was approaching her ninetieth birthday – almost voted against it. The three negative votes were cast by the former president (who launched the attack), the former vice president (man barking) and the Board member who was frightened by a cat forty years earlier.

The former president then approached me and said, "I never had anything against your cat, and I even voted for cats during the pet amendment. I looked at her dumbstruck, but chose not to say a word. Pandemonium broke out. It was finally over.

I wish to give my Qualified Representative the next to last word in this book – in the hopes that he will one day be played on the big screen by Robert DeNiro or Richard Geere. He wrote to the Arbitrator the following day:

"Sir:

"On behalf of Respondents, the undersigned confirms their consent that inasmuch as the Respondents have effectively prevailed and as Petitioner recognizes their right to keep their pet cat at the [Good Life Condominium], as they have contended since the beginning, the Amended Petition in this case should be dismissed and the scheduled Final Hearing should be canceled.

"The Petitioner's action on the evening of February 27th, when the Board of Directors passed a resolution which, according to counsel for Petitioner, "grandfathered in all persons with pets as of yesterday's date," effectively granted Respondents the relief they were seeking in this case.

"Petitioner's action was clear recognition that Petitioner's claims against Respondents were baseless, and that Petitioner would never prevail if the matter came to a Final Hearing. Respondents are, however, disappointed that this matter has gone on since September 2004, when they were first sent a "notice" to remove a pet cat that they were entitled to keep.

Defend Your Condo & Homeowner Rights!

"This is a case that should never have been brought. It was an absurd case from the very beginning, apparently launched insensibly by two members of the Board on a "frolic" of their own. It caused great damage to the association and to the Starr family, who have been victimized by the action. All the Unit Owners at the [Good Life Condominium] have suffered from this action, both financially and otherwise.

"Members of the Board have been so distracted by this case since November 2004 that urgent problems at the [Good Life Condominium] have not received proper attention.

"The Starr family has paid an even heavier price, both financially and in terms of the stress and aggravation caused them, not to mention the huge drain on all of our time over nearly one and one half years."

Thanks to my Qualified Representative's dedicated efforts, we won the moral victory, our costs were reimbursed and my Little Guy's tale inspired the first Condo and Homeowner Defense Kit and Education Service.

"The best way out of a problem is through it."

– Anonymous

Afterword

Chess Master Mikhail Tal once pointed out that "Life is like chess. Either you win or you learn." I hope, dear reader, that you were able to learn the easy way by reading this book, rather than suffering through the harsh experiences described.

Assuming that you chose the former, you can also further your education with the companion books in our **Condo & HOA Defense Kit**: *Condo Board Revolt* and *Creating Condo & Home Owner Association Documents*.

The Defense Kit includes indispensable guidance on:

♦   Condo and Homeowner Board Abuse;

♦   Legal Enforcement Actions;

♦   Elections and Recalls; and

♦   Association Documents.

The Defense Kit can be life-changing, if not life-saving, for concerned and distraught condo or HOA members.

Defend Your Condo & Homeowner Rights!

The **Condo & HOA Education Service** provides teleseminars and web-based training (webinars) for :

> * Present or prospective Board members, real estate attorneys, realtors, community managers, trainers and non-profit organizations;
>
> * Review and refinement of association documents for law firms; and
>
> * Specialized services as required.

For further information about the Condo & HOA Defense Kit and Educational service, please visit our website (www.DrJoyceStarr.com) or contact: info@drjoycestarr.com.

"Too much of a good thing is wonderful."

– Mae West

Defend Your Condo & Homeowner Rights!

Index

Defend Your Condo & Homeowner Rights!

Special Appreciation to
TExtract © Texyz 2007
www.Texyz.com

Defend Your Condo & Homeowner Rights!

About the Author

Dr. Joyce Starr is an author, publisher and policy expert.

She established her niche publishing house in 2006. Dr. Joyce STARR Publishing specializes in books that Empower and Inspire, (www.DrJoyceStarr.com).

In 2007, she authored and published: *Defend Your Condo & Homeowner Rights!: What You Must Do When the Board Turns Your Life Upside Down*. She also created the first Condo and HOA Defense Kit.

Dr. Starr has authored books in diverse arenas, including: international policy, environmental policy, public policy and dynamic wellness strategies. Harper Collins, Henry Holt, Praeger and Contemporary Books published her works.

Her commentaries have appeared in leading newspapers – including the *Washington Post, Washington Times, Miami Herald, LA Times, International Herald Tribune* and *Jerusalem Post* – and numerous online media. She has given over a thousand radio and television interviews.

Defend Your Condo & Homeowner Rights!

Dr. Starr has designed programs and centers of excellence for prominent think tanks and universities. Director of the Near East Program of the Center for Strategic and International Studies (CSIS) in Washington, D.C., she undertook groundbreaking projects on the Middle East peace process and produced acclaimed works on critical water shortages in the region. She also organized three global water summits, serving as co-chair with the UN Secretary General and with heads of state.

Secretary of the Task Force for the Reconstruction of Lebanon, she also created an online database for reconstruction contracts abroad.

A communications expert, Dr. Starr served as chairman of the Communications Department of Mount Vernon College and dealt with public policy outreach as a member of the White House staff.

She consults with firms in cutting-edge arenas.

By the Author

Condo & Homeowner Defense Series

Defend Your Condo & Homeowner Rights!
What You Must Do When the Board
Turns Your Life Upside Down

The Condo Commandos 101 Reality eBook

Living Younger Series

Ancient Artisan Salt:
A Journey to Your Salt Solution

Himalayan Crystals:
Your Dynamic Wellness Guide

Inspirational Series

Faxes to God:
Messages to the Western Wall of Jerusalem

International Series

Covenant Over Middle Eastern Waters:
Key to World Survival

149

Defend Your Condo & Homeowner Rights!

*Kissing Through Glass: The Invisible Shield
Between Americans and Israelis*

US Policy on Water Resources in the Middle East

*A Shared Destiny: Near East
Reconstruction and Development*

CPSIA information can be obtained at www.ICGtesting.com
Printed in the USA
LVOW080314070412

276587LV00007B/93/A